INSTRUCTOR'S MANUAL

Creating the

Writing
Portfolio

INSTRUCTOR'S MANUAL

Creating the

Writing Portfolio

Alan J. Purves
Joseph A. Quattrini
Christine I. Sullivan

 NTC *Publishing Group*
Lincolnwood, Illinois USA

Published by NTC Publishing Group.
© 1995 by NTC Publishing Group, 4255 West Touhy Avenue,
Lincolnwood (Chicago), Illinois 60646-1975 U.S.A.
Manufactured in the United States of America.

4 5 6 7 8 9 0 VP 9 8 7 6 5 4 3 2 1

CONTENTS

Introduction

ABOUT THE TEXTBOOK

The three authors of the book, Chris, Joe, and Alan, teach writing in Connecticut and New York. We came together as a result of a research project examining the use of portfolios in the literature class, but we see little real separation of reading and writing, literature and composition. What began as a somewhat skeptical look at a bandwagon has given us a sense that the portfolio approach represents a sea change in writing instruction. When we were approached by the publisher to do a book on portfolios and writing, we leaped at the opportunity.

The book we have produced is somewhat different from some writing textbooks. We have decided to approach student readers as we do our own students. They are individuals needing to take responsibility for themselves and their lives and careers as writers. We want to take them seriously. We want them to take their writing seriously. This manual is our way of helping you, their instructors, to approach the textbook and your students in this frame of mind.

In writing the textbook, then, we saw ourselves as engaged in a conversation with student writers. We are not their instructor. You are. You know them better than we can. You have the direct responsibility for assigning their writing, looking at the drafts, encouraging conversations, reviews, and revisions, and grading and judging their work and their worth as students. What we intend in the textbook is to provide students with some guidelines for engaging in the activity of creating a writing portfolio.

ABOUT THIS INSTRUCTOR'S GUIDE

This instructor's guide is just that, a guide. A guidebook does not tell you what to do every step of the journey; neither does this book seek to make you dependent on what we have done and where we have been. You will not find a detailed lesson plan in these pages. Instead you will find a general map of the teaching of writing using a portfolio approach and several suggestions for what to take along and what to do. Writing courses should be dependent on you and your students: where *you* are, who *you* are, what *you* want to do. The textbook and the guide are there to help you and to orient you and your students in thinking about writing and the teaching and learning of writing. We will include some general theoretical considerations about portfolios and about writing and then spend some time going through the major task of teaching—making assignments and marking and grading compositions.

ABOUT THE PURPOSE OF PORTFOLIOS

A writing portfolio is not the same as a folder of student writing; it is a deliberate effort to present oneself to the outside world as a writer or a student of writing. A writing folder is *third*-person, *passive* voice. Instructor selects, instructor collects, instructor decides. A portfolio, on the other hand, is *first*-person, *active* voice. The writer sets goals, makes selections, makes decisions. How one does this is the focus of this book. It can and should also be the focus of a writing course, not for the sake of the creation of a portfolio, but for what the portfolio will show about the student. Our purpose as instructors of writing is to help students prepare themselves as independent writers and to give them a sense of their strength and their potential. The idea behind the portfolio approach is responsibility and the ways in which you can help your students become responsible for their writing and become responsible writers. If you are to give them responsibility, so we must give you responsibility.

ORGANIZATION OF THE TEXTBOOK

The textbook is divided into eight chapters. These chapters are arranged for reading from the beginning to the end of the course, but they can also be used as a handbook at various stages in the course.

Chapter 1 introduces the idea of portfolios in writing and shows the student some possibilities for planning the working and presentation portfolios.

Chapter 2 deals with getting started in writing and outlines the planning and drafting stage of the writing process.

Chapter 3 goes into further detail on academic writing, particularly in English classes, and explores some of the concepts of style in writing.

Chapter 4 looks at writing across the curriculum and shows how the portfolio can be built up with a variety of writing activities.

Chapter 5 explores writing about literature as a particular feature of writing in English classes.

Chapter 6 deals with revision and takes the student through the steps of revision, including revision for the portfolio.

Chapter 7 explores editing and the preparation of the final copy of an individual paper.

Chapter 8 returns to the portfolio and takes up the preparation of the presentation portfolio.

The Appendix presents some reference data and advice on grammar and style.

Each chapter includes a preview, a summary, and a discussion of the use of computers in writing.

The volume is arranged, therefore, to take students through the process of preparing a portfolio. It does not prescribe the portfolio nor does it prescribe individual writing assignments. We suggest some here and there throughout the book, but it has been our experience that the best writing assignments grow out of the class itself. Even a really good written or photographic prompt needs to be adapted to the type of students who are in the class and to the particular teaching situation of that day or week. We can and do provide guidelines for assignments in this guide, but we believe that the actual assignment must be yours so that the writing becomes your students', not yours or ours.

Good writing comes out of reading, observation, experience, and discussion. The writing course can be a course in literature, history, politics, sociology, art, comics, pop music, the environment. It might include topics from all these fields or topics selected from them by theme or interest.

Although the appendix deals with those issues of grammar and style that we think make the most difference between writing and good writing, the textbook is not a handbook.

We believe the book should be supplemented by a good dictionary, a solid handbook on usage, a thesaurus, a collection of materials to read (possibly in an anthology), and such books as Natalie Goldberg's *Writing Down the Bones* or William Stafford and Stephen Dunning's *Getting the Knack*, two excellent books of exercises for writers by writers. Mostly, we think the writing should come out of your work with your students.

ORGANIZATION OF THIS INSTRUCTOR'S GUIDE

This volume has six chapters. Chapter 1 sets forth our understanding of the portfolio approach to writing. Chapter 2 gives a theoretical view of writing and the writing classroom, with a particular emphasis on the use of computers in composition. Chapter 3 goes into the setting of goals and standards. Chapter 4 takes up the writing assignment. In Chapter 5, there is a discussion of grading and marking. Chapter 6 discusses the evaluation of portfolios.

In this guide, then, we shall not march you through the volume in traditional fashion, but we shall discuss various topics about portfolios and writing. We think it is important to set forth an approach to the teaching of writing that is consistent and humane. We want to explain something about writing and also deal with the nuts and bolts. There is then, a bit more on "why" than there is on "what" or "how." The what and the how are contained in the student volume.

ACKNOWLEDGMENTS

We want to give special thanks to our colleagues in the portfolio project: Deane Beverley, Maria Fusco, Marion Galbraith, Rich Harris, John Hennelly, Suzanne Heyd, Gertrude Karabas, Ann Kuthy, Nancy Lester, Carol Mackin, Carol Mohrman, Charles Phelps, Sarah Jordan, and Kathleen Sims. We only hope we haven't disappointed them.

Chapter 1   What a Focus on the Portfolio Approach Means

Portfolios are not just nice, they are, in fact, necessary to the teaching of English and composition. Portfolios provide you with the luxury of exploring writing with your students and watching them take responsibility for their own learning. For the past year and a half, we have been part of a group of teachers (in junior and senior high schools and four-year colleges in New York and Connecticut) developing portfolios for ascertaining literature learning in their classrooms. From our own work and from observing and sharing with colleagues who teach students of many different backgrounds, levels of previous performance in writing, and levels of interest in school and academic work, we have arrived at the following general principles:

1. A portfolio is meant to present the student to the outside world.
2. A portfolio should seek to reflect the breadth of the student's accomplishments.
3. A portfolio should seek to justify the particular course or curriculum that the student has undertaken.
4. A portfolio should be the responsibility of the student.
5. A portfolio has a rhetorical purpose: to inform and to persuade.
6. Creating a portfolio is a form of formative evaluation; the portfolio itself, on the other hand, serves as a summative evaluation.

We shall now expand upon these general principles by providing some context and specific details.

1. A portfolio is meant to present the student to the outside world. In the professional world, a portfolio is what an artist or a business person takes to the prospective employer or client. It is the first glimpse that many people have of that person. In some ways, a portfolio is an amplified résumé. It seeks to show the person off to the world, to say, "Look! Here is what I have done that may serve as an indicator of what I can do." It includes things that the person has created or helped to create, and it contains comments on and/or reviews of those things.

So too it should be in an academic setting. The portfolio is not a mere collection of papers or drafts of papers. It is not an internal document for the student and teacher alone. It should seek to contain those items that best represent the accomplishments of the student to a broader world. Some of the items may be things that have been assigned, but some may be freely chosen. What you and your students might seek to develop is the sense of the importance of the portfolio. It is the demonstration of people's performance as students of writing—as keyboarders, writers, talkers, document designers, and artists. It should show what they know, what they can do, and what they do on their own.

Because the portfolio is a demonstration of performance, questions arise about what should be included. Many people have insisted that a succession of drafts should be in a student's portfolio. We are not sure why a series of rehearsals must be included with the performance. One may assume that the person has rehearsed or not rehearsed by the performance itself. What do the drafts tell us? Whether the student did the work without help? Not really. Whether the student understood the feedback? Perhaps. That the instructor encouraged revision? Probably. That the student cares about the quality of the writing? Yes, but that can be seen just as well in the final version. We think that the issue of drafts raises the further question of the purpose the portfolio serves. At one time, it serves a formative function and remains an internal document to the class to be gone over by students and instructor. At another time, however, it serves a summative purpose and provides evidence to the outside world of the accomplishments of students and the class (and by implication the instructor). Drafts well serve the internal purpose; they are of a special value to the external purpose, as we shall explain in the next section on practice. We shall return to this point at the end.

Another way to think of the portfolio is as a portrait. Any portrait is taken from an angle. And the angle of the portrait may vary from student to student and class to class. In the courses that we have been observing, one kind of portrait is a portrait of mastery, proving to the students and the world that they are indeed competent individuals. Another kind of portrait appears in the courses where one kind of mastery is replaced by another, the so-called "creative writing" class where mastery is seen in artistic rather than workaday terms. In other courses, the angle of the portrait is that of growth and change over a period of time. In still others it is a portrait of the student as a member of an intellectual or rhetorical community. In most courses, it is a portrait of the student as a responsible human being, capable of both working independently and being part of a group (the relative importance of these two naturally depends upon the purposes and philosophy of the course).

A third way of thinking about a portfolio is as a room in a museum or gallery. How are the pieces to be arranged? What direction should the viewer turn in order to get the best view? There are other metaphors that instructors have employed, including a rite of passage into maturity and independence, an exhibition, an autobiography, and a map.

2. A portfolio should seek to reflect the breadth of the student's accomplishments. Writing instruction, however it is conceived (whether as process- or product-oriented, whether focusing on collaborative or individual work, whether general or specialized), includes three major components that should probably be represented in a portfolio: knowledge, practice, and habits. The precise mix depends upon the approach and the goals of the particular program. However conceived, writing instruction demands that the students do something, produce something.

Knowledge is divided into that which is contained in texts, the content of the instruction or the subject, the nature of texts, and the ways of producing texts. It includes knowledge of conventions like spelling and grammar and of genres. We shall discuss the role of knowledge in Chapter 2.

Practice is perhaps the heart of the writing curriculum; it is, after all, what people do—write essays, stories, plays, poems, compositions of all sorts. But since the practice is studied, thinking about the practice is part of the curriculum as well. Like any academic subject, composition involves public acts in which the student must be more articulate about procedures and strategies as well as conclusions than might be true outside of the academy. Proofs are often not necessary in mathematical applications outside of academic contexts; essays about one's reading of a text are not required after reading every library book. A portfolio may need to contain evidence of articulated understanding of writing, extended responses such as process notes, writer's diaries, and drafts. All of these serve to indicate that the practice is studied and conscious, that the students have thought about what they are doing. Raw talent is usually not enough.

Habits refers broadly to the set of attitudes, stances, and beliefs that we encourage through formal or informal instruction. We teach students to do such things as check for spelling, go to a peer response group, or make an outline so as to instill in them habits that they will adopt as their own. Individuals do some things as a matter of conscious volition; other things they do by habit. They are disposed to do those things, and educational institutions reinforce and direct those dispositions.

The academic writer exists in a field of composition study that has developed in that writer a set of habits of mind about how to write and how to talk about what has been written. Habits are a necessary part of our having an educational system and our being a society. They are what tie us together as a culture of writers and readers; they are not to be attacked in the name of individualism. As instructors, we should be more conscious about the habits that we teach than we have been, and we should take pride in our success as well as raise concerns about what we are doing. Our students practice and learn how to perform a particular kind of writing, and they are encouraged to write this way voluntarily. Once it was thought that the five-paragraph theme should become a habit. Now it is believed that the steps of planning, drafting, revising, and editing should become habitual. At the same time, attention to certain aspects of structure, form, and content is also seen as a desirable habit in writers. Our grading and marking practices instill habits of thinking about their writing that stay with our students throughout their lives. Many instructors have generated the habit of worrying about spelling and usage so much that the students become stifled in their writing and generating of ideas. Habits can be healthy or unhealthy, and we must be aware of what habits we are fostering.

This last set of habits that we inculcate can have its positive side. Our comments on student papers serve as a guide to them as to how to judge their own writing and that of others and how to justify these judgments publicly. When we mark and comment upon student writing, we should do so with the expectation that the students will "internalize" our criteria and use them on their writing and that of their peers before they even hand it in. Since language education is supposed to develop something called "taste" or the love of "good writing," the curriculum looks beyond reading and writing to the formation of specific sets of preferences and habits of reading and writing. It may include the development of a tolerance for the variety of styles and an acceptance that just because we do not like a certain text does not mean that it is not good. The development of such habits of mind should lead students to the rejection of the meretricious and the acceptance of cultural diversity in writing and, by extension, in society. These are often cited as parts of the curriculum in academic literature, but they loom less large in the minds of students and instructors because they are not part of the assessed curriculum; in addition, we know less about how to handle the student who is recalcitrant in these habits. We do seek some sort of an indication of how these habits are developing when we ask for the self-statement or critical introduction to the student's own work.

The academic curriculum can also lead students to developing a taste based on an awareness of the meretricious or shoddy use of sentiment or language. Experienced readers and writers can see that they are being tricked by a book or a film even when the trickery is going on—and they can enjoy the experience. Like advertising and propaganda, literature manipulates the reader or viewer. The conscious student can be aware of such manipulation and value the craft at the same time as discerning the motives that lie behind it.

Since the curriculum seeks to promote habits of mind in writing and habits of writing, there must be multiple samples of student responses in order to see what aspects of them have become habitual. That is why we need a portfolio in the first place. A single essay or a single test does not tell us enough about the habits of mind of our students; only a portfolio can do that.

The portfolio should seek to capture all of those aspects of a writing curriculum and the performance of students in academic writing as they reflect the aims and standards set by the community, the institution, and the course. That is the main reason why we do not tell you or the students what we think should be in a portfolio. That is up to you. We try to help you make those decisions, but they are ultimately between you and your students.

A portfolio must be a comprehensive record of the student in the context of the school and the course, a portrait including many facets. Portfolios represent the curriculum in practice, not a set of abstractions. To make what we have outlined concrete, instructors should ask themselves the following questions:

1. What do I look for in student writing and performance?
2. What do I accept as evidence?
3. What do I see as being better? As being older or more mature?
4. What do I want to communicate about the students and the course? To whom?

The answers must be particular to the course to have any validity at all. We shall return to these questions in Chapters 3, 4, and 5.

3. A portfolio should seek to justify the particular course or curriculum that the student has undertaken. This may seem odd, but the point is simple. The portfolio should seek to reflect what the goals and functions of the courses have been. It should serve to reflect what we have been teaching, and what goals the school has set for the students. A portfolio should be neither a collection of scores on commercial tests nor items on a behavioral checklist provided by a commercial or state agency (although a sample of these might be included in a portfolio). It should, we think, contain a statement of the goals and aims of the course and the school. Thus, anyone looking at the portfolio should be able to reconstruct the writing program that the student has had and should know what its objectives and criteria were. The portfolio may well also include a list of the opportunities provided by the school for students to participate in activities related to writing—a student magazine or a school newspaper, for example.

4. A portfolio should be the responsibility of the student. This is the opposite side of the tenet we just set forth, and it is equally simple. A portfolio should be created by the students. It may have guidelines from the school or the instructor about the kinds of things that might be included (or must be included), such as a number of kinds of writing, a self-evaluation, or a number of original compositions or performances (film, music, writing). But the decision as to what specific pieces should be included and how they should be included should remain the students'. They must also work out how best to put group work into the portfolio. If they cooperate on a project that involves the building of a model, they might have to use photographs. If there is a dramatization, there must be an audiotape or a videotape. If there is a really good discussion or collaboration in writing, they must figure out how to put that into the portfolio to show why it is good and what part they took in it. The students are laying themselves on the line, perhaps before the whole school or before a jury of instructors. It is their choice as to whether they should be seen as uncaring slobs or as people who take pride in their work. Instructors cannot do this for them. By taking responsibility for what they show of themselves to the world, students have a new power that they don't have when they are simply handing assignments in and getting grades. It takes time for students to realize that they are not helpless, that they earn the grade or the rating, you do not give it to them. We have found that students become quite good in judging their own worth. There are a few who don't get the point, who think that just because they did it they deserve a good grade. Most come to see a difference between doing it and doing it for a portfolio that is a public document.

One way of encouraging this responsibility is to use the technique of "grouping." This is a form of reflection that has been used in other contexts and that works in schools (we explain it to the students in Chapter 1 of the student volume). It depends upon having the members of the group use the same format each time they meet. The format is usually one of questions about how the members of the group are progressing toward a set of goals that they have defined. The group members share their answers to those questions each time, talk with each other about them, and encourage each other. It is a time of sharing and reflection, generally not one of admonition or assessment (other than self-assessment). What goes on in the group is confidential. It would work in an English course this way. The students would divide into groups of three (the groups would remain together for the year). Every two weeks, the students in a group would get together for a half hour and share their answers to the following questions.

What do I know that I didn't know?
What can I do that I couldn't do?

What do I do that I didn't do?

With respect to each question, the students should be encouraged to make an individual or collective plan and refer their answers to that plan. The grouping is among the students. The instructor does not participate or even know what the plan of the groups might be. That should come out in the portfolio itself. Grouping is a way of having the students look at themselves and learn how they can take responsibility for their own learning. It is simple, and it works.

5. A portfolio has a rhetorical purpose: to inform and to persuade. Again, this point sums up much of what we have gone over before. The portfolio should inform the observer as to what students have done in the particular writing course. It should reflect the breadth and depth of the course and the experiences it contains. Since it is public, it should be understandable to the outside world and, perhaps, conform to certain principles:

1. *The portfolio should tell what has been studied.* It should reflect the curriculum of a course and of the school and the broader interests of the student. It need not do this chronologically, although that is often a possible organization. It might be organized by groups or classes of activity (papers, discussions, dramatizations).

2. *The portfolio should convey the value of what has been studied.* It should seek to show why it is important to have done what was done, to include what was included, to be judged by the standards that have been established. It should have some sort of introduction and commentary, perhaps by the student, perhaps by the course, perhaps even by some outside juror.

3. *The portfolio should convey the merit of the individual student.* The portfolio should attempt to show that this student has done as well as he or she has by saying something about change or growth, or about breadth, or about mastery, or about knowledge.

One thing that these principles suggest is that a portfolio cannot be slapped together. It should make a good first impression as well as reinforce a strong second and third impression. Like any composition, a portfolio is known by its content, its arrangement, and its style. A portfolio is to a composition as a book is to a chapter or as a hypertext is to any of its components. And a portfolio takes time; it is not the work of the night before. It will probably take most of a week every quarter to review portfolios with students. But don't begrudge the time, for the students will have gained in depth of understanding what they might have lost in the one short story that would have been covered.

6. Creating a portfolio is a form of formative evaluation; the portfolio itself, on the other hand, serves as a summative evaluation. This is a tricky point, and perhaps the most difficult for students and instructors. During the course of our teaching writing, we act as the coach, the person who encourages the students to bring out their best, who elicits responses, discussion, and ideas and feelings. These may come out in discussions, in drafts of papers, in rehearsals of various sorts. We are generally friendly creatures, helpful beasts in the traditional quest stories. There comes a time, however, when we must drop that role, when the students are showing their stuff for real, when they have to confront the dragon, and we are the dragon-judge. This is hard for many of us and for our students. But it is a shift in role that we must acknowledge in ourselves and explain to our students.

What we said about the drafts to encourage pride and revision cannot be said about the final product. We are the judge (unless we can get someone else to take on that role); we are the expert who can describe the performance of students and hold it up against standards that we have set. We have to cast off our mantle of friendliness and look through the lens of the critic or the judge. This is not an inhumane act at all; it is an act of love, and we should try to help our students understand it. We can no longer be the parent/advocate, the attorney for the defense. We cannot rationalize our students' work; it must stand on its own. That is the point at which our students become independent of us, and it is a point towards which we must lead them so that they can be free of us and autonomous. We think it is the hardest part of teaching, but probably the most important, and if you take anything away from this manual, we hope that this point is the one that remains. We are seeking to help our students to become independent, responsible human beings who no longer need us. To effect this end, we need to balance our tendency to do things for the students with our tendency to serve as the judge. This duality is the crux of the portfolio approach; it is also the crux of what it means to be a teacher. The fact of portfolios encourages us to face ourselves as teachers and as human beings for the education (the leading away from childhood) of our students.

Chapter 2   What Are We about When We Teach Writing and Literacy in the Digital Age?

We teach in an age in which many of the older notions about writing and reading have been changed, primarily by the electronic and digital revolutions. Where before people found it necessary to write letters, they can now telephone or send a fax or e-mail. Where before people read books and newspapers, they can now listen to the radio, watch television, or go on-line with a computerized bulletin board. Where before people wrote by hand or used a typewriter, they now use their personal computers. Each of these technological changes has forced us to reconsider the ways by which we communicate and what is meant by such terms as *writing* and *literacy*. Technological advances have certainly changed what goes on in our classrooms. We think it necessary to explore some of these changes, which are in part responsible for the new emphasis on the portfolio.

Writing and literacy involve the use of various technologies (currently, the computer and the book or screen). They also involve using these technologies within a social or cultural framework (people read and write in a specific city or country, and they read or write letters or articles or lists). A technical definition of literacy would have it that those who are marginally literate are those who approach the lower end of the spectrum in having no technical ability—they are what is called *dysfunctional* or *dyslexic*. From our experience with many such people, we can say that they are able to maneuver in a world of literacy and text, but they cannot master it. They can function in a literate world (can handle McDonalds and check-out counters and *TV Guide*), but they are not literate in the sense of having control over that world and its social structures. They are excluded from many of the literate communities that constitute the "scribal society"—those who control our literate culture by their writing, editing, and handling of written information (and other media, including the electronic ones).

The people who are now considered good at literacy and writing are the people who know their way around books and other print materials, who are able to use a computer to generate different kinds of texts, who are able to manipulate the images on the screen as well as to work with the yellow pad and pencil and the library or database. They have acquired a vast body of knowledge, and they can use this knowledge to play with language and writing. These people are to writing what the Nintendo expert is to the visual and motor screen. They play with and manipulate pieces of text rather than try to set ideas down on paper. They are engaged in the world of what is now called *hypertext*, the multi-authored, shifting electronic text that is made up of images on the screen. This is a different world from that of pencil and paper, yet at the same time there are some clear connections.

When we embark on using the computer in writing instruction, how do we explore with the students the fact that they are engaged in working with a multi-author hypertext? They are there to enter their draft, let's say, but then they need to realize that within the chips are some other authors: a formatter, a speller, a grammarian, an organizer, a production specialist. They can also access a database, perhaps, or use graphics or sound in their production. They can work with all of these, do their part, and then say, "OK, speller, you have a go at it." They are already doing collaborative writing. They can bring in another human too, if they are networked, or even if they take their disk to another person. The writer with the computer is never alone. How does using these power tools alter writers, change the nature of writing and of the text, or change the ways in which novices and experts understand these matters? Should they trust their invisible colleagues? What is left for them?

Electronic technology also brings us to consider how we envision the process of writing. The traditional terminology of planning, drafting, revising, and editing may no longer be appropriate or may need to be reconstrued. The fact that we can store text on a disk means that we may leave it at any time and return to it at any other. But the program takes us back to the beginning of the text each time. We are thus invited to begin again or to revise what we have written before we go on to the next part. It is also difficult to be sure when we have completed a draft. We are never sure whether the segment we wrote today will go in one composition only or be reused as a part of another. The very finite nature of the book or the text has disappeared. We are like the painter returning to the studio rather than like the musician returning to the score or the cook returning to the kitchen to prepare yet another meal. But that analogy is not truly appropriate either. Today's finished portrait is tomorrow's sketch. Space and time are rearranged in the new configuration of text and hypertext. Do we have a pedagogy that helps us to deal with this new sense of text and change and completion?

How do we help students who are both scared of texts and unsure of the new machinery? What are the best means of helping students work through the cycle of production of a finished text? How do we get them to work out their own modus operandi? We ourselves are too new as members of this electronic world, a world that is changing as we move from idea to finished text. The world of hypermedia and the world of electronic bulletin boarding is changing the nature of composition before our very senses. It seems a barely manageable world, where the forms of text and the forms of text production are in flux. How can we begin to think of what it is that is "basic" or where to begin with students?

Perhaps we should think of ourselves as introducing students to a technology, a program. Perhaps we should see our students as needing to consider both the models of academic writing and the tools for making those models real.

Writing on the computer, even more blatantly than earlier forms of writing, involves the moving around of images. It is an act of visual composition and arrangement. We do not manipulate words (things with meaning) or graphemes (signs of things with meaning) as much as we manipulate segments of space (which contain graphic signs of things with meaning). Our manipulation takes place in no-space (not on a page or a sheet of paper or a scroll), but on a simulacrum of space. Our manipulation is of intangibles. Eventually, they may become tangible.

Students can become fairly adept at this kind of composition, but it is a new composition, one that deals with arrangement and playful rearrangement as much as it deals with the generation of language for ideas. It is a way of composition to which many of us are newcomers, and we are trying to work with our students as instructors must have done with students who were learning writing in the days of the early printing press: They still practiced monastic copying when that was no longer the problem that writers faced. It took about two hundred years for people to realize that copying was not composition. Now we must realize that "writing" is not composition, at least composition as we practice it. We live in an age where composing and playing with the images of text, sound, and picture have taken on a radically new cast.

Composition, then, is manipulation of images for a rhetorical effect. The images are not only the traditional graphemes, punctuation marks, and paragraphs; they are typefaces, illustrations, and sound effects, a complex arrangement of digitized information. They can include the digitized re-creation of an opera, a computer-enhanced image of its set, the libretto, and a bibliography, all of which have been accessed through the Internet. The act of composition is the act of creation or re-creation from a multitude of sources (including the writer's head). In this world, we are all neophytes, although some artists and a few rhetoricians have been looking at the manipulation of images for the past thirty years. Our lead in teaching composition may well come from the concrete poets, the makers of comic books, and the designers of Las Vegas and other spaces, as well as from the rhetoricians who have kept up with them, people such as Richard Lanham.

The fact that writing is now the manipulation of images and the creation of multiple texts lends itself to the idea of the portfolio, where the students can show off their wares and the variety of their creations. They can show off what they know, what they can do, and what habits they have developed.

THE ROLE OF KNOWLEDGE

One way to begin to think of the new writer is to start with knowledge. We can say that good writers possess the following kinds of knowledge:

1. *A portion of the information that is to be encoded or decoded.* They know the vocabulary of what they are reading and writing about—probably as much as 75 percent of it—before they begin to read or to write. More importantly, they also know databases and sources of text, image, and sound, so that they can organize or assemble their composition.

2. *The graphic symbols that encode and structure that information (e.g., the alphanumeric system, punctuation, paragraphing, and document design).* They can recognize complex text forms from simple stimuli—such as seeing pale orange newsprint and recognizing it as a financial newspaper. As writers, they know some of these traditional symbols as well as some of the new symbols of punctuation that are used on the Internet and the symbols of a visual culture that is filled with logos and icons.

3. *The techniques for encoding and decoding using an appropriate technology (from a crayon to a computer).* They can select appropriate technologies for their work or recognize the technologies that have been used to generate some of the material from which they shape their compositions.

4. *Genres or text-types and their uses, including models of successful text types (e.g., the differences between shopping lists and business letters).* They know what these genres look like and how long they are expected to be, as well as what purposes different genres serve. They are aware of the effects of mixing genres and of bringing media together.

5. *The functions of text-types in storing or communicating information, including the relative social utility and importance of these text-types, and the appropriate ways to approach and use these types as information (e.g., the difference between real mail and junk mail).* They know what to do with the variety of texts that are presented them in their environment, and they know what text and media forms best serve their immediate and long-range purposes.

These five areas of knowledge undergird all writing, particularly writing in the age of the computer and of hypertext and digital media. The most adept writer can employ this array of knowledge in a variety of activities—commercial, religious, cultural, communal, and domestic—and do so in a manner that is seen as appropriate to each situation. The adept writer is not only articulate with written language and text but fluent and socially appropriate as well. What appears to guide the adept writer is having a complex array of mental models of the functions and forms of written discourse (by discourse we mean text that can be seen as containing information; a computer keyboard is not discourse but a shopping list or a text space on the screen is). Having these, he or she can proceed to read or write; not having these in their full complexity, he or she is forced to live on the margins of an information society.

THE FRAMEWORK OF LITERATE MODELS

When people write and read, they engage in an activity that is bounded to some extent by existing models of text and behavior toward text. We prefer the word *models* because it suggests the strong visual basis to whatever it is that drives and controls our literacy. Writing and hypertext are primarily visual means of handling language. They involve the manipulation of images of words, phrases, sentences, paragraphs, and even larger chunks of pixels on a screen. What we write we write to be seen, and what we write is somehow determined by the picture in our head of what the final version should "look like." Of course we may experiment with models and mix them up (as is now happening with the "hypermedia" or mixed-media productions).

These models are dictated by people's previous experience of actual written texts, including sounds and images (those they have seen in their environment and those to which they have been exposed through instruction, particularly in school), and the ways in which those texts were handled by others. Our imagination is somehow limited by our previous experience, although a few people can make truly original combinations and compositions. These models in space and in the head determine the habits of a literate society and help form the culture surrounding writers and readers. They help us recognize that "This is a poem," "This is an advertisement," or "This is a well-written composition." These models of text have formal properties, as we shall see, but those forms are or were driven by the functions of text in a given community. At times, the forms cease to be functional and either remain vestigial or are replaced (like "archaic" spellings or the opening of business letters—"Yours of the 21st received ...").

The variation in forms of writing and imaging follows from a variation in what people perceive as the various functions of texts and literacy in a community. These perceptions can be divided into three aspects. The first of these aspects is the relative stress given to the functions of discourse (speech, writing, and the visual and musical arts):

1. *expressive* of the writer (the diary or the love letter);
2. *referential* to the external world (the report or the newspaper article);
3. *conative* or persuasive to the reader (the advertisement or the editorial);
4. *metalingual* or about the medium itself (the dictionary definition or the thesaurus);
5. *poetic* or to serve aesthetic ends (the story, poem, or play);
6. *phatic* to maintain a link between writer and reader (the picture postcard or the greeting card).

All of the writing and composition that people do is based on one or some combination of these functions. Sometimes they are practiced on purpose and in isolation; sometimes they are combined.

The second kind of variation that shapes the function of writing we may think of as the cognitive demand of the discourse, which is to say the degree to which the writer must "invent" either the content of the written text, the form of the text, or both, or to which the reader must note or more deeply ponder it. Written language can range from transcription through organization or reorganization of material known to the writer to invention or generation of both content and form or structure. Reading can range from recognition to following procedures to interpretation or evaluation.

The third kind of variation concerns the social function of the writing: Who is to write, when, and for what audience and who is to read what with what intended outcome. This function may also limit or expand the readership of the writing (at least at first). A love letter excludes many people that a classified advertisement would not. The former involves one person at the writing end and one at the reading end (although in some societies there may be scribes or other intervenors); the latter involves several writers to produce the final text and presumably a large number of readers. Social function also determines the amount of time spent upon the writing or reading, the occasion when the writing or the reading is to take place, the relative importance of content, organization, and even spelling, and the assumed or intended outcome of the text, which includes the subsequent actions of the writer and the reader.

These three social and intellectual functions interact with each other in any given situation; this interaction in turn affects the text produced by changing the mental model (or the picture in the head of what the finished piece of writing "should" look like) held by the writer. In other words, writing a letter in a business setting to a colleague differs from writing to the same colleague from home. Writing a personal narrative differs from writing the explanation of how to prepare a favorite dish (although both follow a chronological line). Writing a story for one's child differs from writing for unknown children in school, and the stories may differ as well. Academic literacy, in particular, differs greatly from nonacademic literacy and has a unique set of constraints and models. In school and college, literate acts must be put on display through talk or action, and school texts and reading and writing have their peculiar forms and structures (many of which are challenged by the new electronic setting).

We would represent the interaction of these aspects of the role of writing as having their effects on text models as in Table 2.1. The three key features that set some sort of bound upon text models are:

1. the amount, type, and mode of presentation (e.g., graphic, sound, pictorial) of information included in a given text;

2. the tools and constituent acts and operations in writing (and, by extension, reading), such as the kinds of implements selected and the surfaces upon which the text is placed and such relevant operations such as spelling, revising, skimming, or criticizing;

3. the formal characteristics of the text, including visual layout, discourse structures, and stylistic devices.

What binds each of these is what binds the functions of writing and reading: convention, which is to say that literate acts are always social acts and as social acts are constrained by the conventional models of a given community. The particular interaction helps to form both rhetorical and interpretive communities.

Table 2.1

A Schematic of the Models Involved in Writing and Being Literate

The Functional Models Governing Written Discourse

Functions of Discourse	Cognitive Demands of Discourse	Social Context of Discourse
Expressive Referential Conative Metalingual Poetic Phatic	Reproducing Reorganizing Organizing Generating	Person Time Occasion Audience Outcome

**These Converge upon and Interact with the Tools and Acts
Involved in Producing a Text**

Surfaces	Inscribing Instruments	Text-producing Acts	Discourse-producing Acts
Paper Screen Tape Other	Manual Mechanical Electronic Other	Inscribing Editing	Drafting Revising

**These Again Converge upon, Influence, and Are Influenced by the
Textual Models that Appear in Any Piece of Writing**

Information	Spatial Characteristics	Structural Characteristics

Amount
Selection
Level of Detail
Perspective
Tone
	Calligraphy/Typeface
	Word Boundaries
	Sentence Boundaries
	Segment Boundaries
	Conventional Units
	Paragraphs
	Address Blocks
	Sections/Chapters
	List Categories
	Subheads
	Tables
	Columns
	Cross-References
	Visuals
	Bold, Italics, etc.
	Figures
	Illustrations
	Quick-Time Video
	Audio
	Other Virtual Devices
		Propositional Patterns
		Temporal
		  Narrative
		  Process
		  Cause/Effect
		Spatial
		  Physical Display
		  Anatomy
		Classificatory
		  Definition
		  Analogy
		  Comparison
		
		Appositional Patterns
		Stream of Consciousness
		Schematic
		Association of Images or
		  Words
		
		Tabular Patterns
		Cross-Referenced Lists

In general, a particular culture or community (a community may best be defined as a subgroup of a larger ethnic or literate culture) determines what models are appropriate and important. The culture surrounding the popular media sees a heavy combination of visual and prose (pictures with captions) as the appropriate model for exposition. This model is very different from that of the scholarly research paper, which in some fields almost prohibits the picture. The fact of cultural variety explains the seeming failure of some people to survive in what to them is an alien community. A student who comes to an academic setting from a workplace where certain kinds of texts are admired will soon find them scorned in an English classroom. So too will a student who does not understand that people are to discuss what they read or that they are to come up with the approved interpretation.

The communities of writers within a country as diverse as the United States may be as distant as the community of loggers and that of urban garment workers, despite the fact that the two may seem similar to an outsider. They even differ in the ways by which they tolerate others' expertise. Writers may hire accountants, because they are not adept in that community; so, too, business executives may hire advertising consultants for their business. They do so without shame or guilt. In many English classrooms, however, hiring a writer or an editor is shrouded in shame and secrecy; the student is to do everything alone.

TOWARDS A FUNCTIONAL RHETORIC

We believe a writing course should employ a rhetoric based not upon speech but upon a full understanding of the new sorts of text. The aspects of the text models that research has made apparent are outlined in Table 2.1. But we would like to spend a bit more time on theory; you may skip this section if you want to get to the how rather than stay with the why and the what.

Clearly, any text has a semantic and propositional content; it is about something, and it presents words and arrangements of words in what is called *discourse*. There may be variation in the amount of information as well as in the selection from the total information on the topic. We may simply write "bread" on a shopping list rather than a minute description of the shape, size, and texture of the bread. On other occasions, full depiction is preferred. There is also variation in the level of abstraction or detail in the text. There is further variation in the perspective from which the material is viewed, the degree of ostensible objectivity of the writing, or the degree to which figurative language is to be employed.

When we turn to form, we should note the emphasis on the visual elements of text. Much of the writing about literacy has focused on the historical and cultural relationship between written and oral language and has suggested that written language differs from conversation but resembles formal oral language in that both use certain stylized and conventional patterns and devices of language so as to make the relationship between speaker and hearer and writer and reader easier to manage. Both types of language are more constrained by convention than is conversational oral language, which relies on the face-to-face interchange of speaker and listener.

We would like to suggest that the distinguishing feature of written language has another antecedent that equally strongly affects it: pictographic representation. Writing can be seen as a descendant from various pictorial or graphic representations of the world of the "painter," such as cave drawings, hieroglyphs and petroglyphs, and various sorts of nonverbal signs and symbol systems. These representations have clearly influenced such aspects of written language as its progression in Western systems from upper left to lower right, its use of size or boldness to indicate emphasis, and its use of white or blank space to indicate divisions between segments. The nature of many of these visual conventions is known to designers, as are the diverse rhetorical effects of typefaces, spacing, illustration, and other graphics. Some of this knowledge seems intuitively held by young readers and writers, manyof whom are adept interpreters of comics and other graphic texts. The visual impact of writing is also clearly seen on the computer screen, where chunks of text may be moved from space to space and be treated as a visual icon rather than a bit of frozen speech. (This moving of chunks can now be done with digitized sound as well, if a person has a synthesizer and the software to do the moving. It can and certainly has been done with shots on a film or videotape.) There has as yet been little serious study by rhetoricians and educators of such matters as the visual conventions in written language, how these conventions are known by writers and readers, and how this knowledge might be used in instruction.

It is apparent that written language or text has the characteristic of segmenting space with print in order to make meaning. Primarily this is done with the use of a set of conventional symbols called *letters*, which are combined into groupings called *words*, which are combined into phrases, sentences, and other units. The spatial segmentation on the page, then, can be seen as demarcating units that have been assigned some sort of meaningfulness. Such is the case with a sentence that can be observed to contain a violation of the conventions of segmentation (such as a typo), and that sort of meaningfulness is often confounded with natural language.

But the meaningfulness of spatial segmentation is much more than the demarcation of word and sentence boundaries. The business letter, the poem, and the newspaper column provide examples of other "shapings" of text in two-dimensional space. The letter and the poem are two obvious examples of text that give a clue as to their meaning from their placement of marks in relation to white space. In addition, they may use another characteristic of written language—such as darkness or letter shape—to give emphasis. Meaning and rhetorical effect can also be portrayed by size of the writing, underlining, and other devices that are peculiar to written format.

Another aspect of the visual presentation of written language that cannot be overlooked is the use of diagrams and illustrations as a part of the total text. These form a clear part of the impression and the meaning in magazines, textbooks, research reports, and other forms of writing, and they are often used in literary writing as well. Such visual forms constitute a part of the text model that helps writers determine when they have achieved the sort of text they have been asked to produce. As more and more is digitized, the visual possibilities increase in the phenomenon known as *hypermedia*. All of these possibilities are available to students.

Beyond these visual aspects of form are the various possible structures of content at either the level of the text or the level of discourse. By the former, we refer to the structure provided in lists and tables; by the latter, to what is traditionally thought of as arrangement or disposition of ideas.

Our students have a long history of experience with the graphic and visual aspects of written texts, primarily through picture books, but also through the environment, including television's presentation of text. In fact, these images of what a text looks like may well exert a dominating effect on early writing and literacy, but curiously they are not made a part of instruction in writing except in the formation of letters and in early penmanship.

The middle element of the models of text is a dual one concerning the production and reception of text. Texts are produced on surfaces, and the particular marks and shapes are created by a variety of instruments that can render two-dimensional or three-dimensional texts. They can be as solid as wooden blocks or neon tubing or as evanescent as a wisp of smoke or a set of pixels on a screen. The people who produce texts both produce the palpable text and discourse. Text-producing acts include the manual act of inscribing and the subsequent act of editing to insure the legibility of the text. Discourse-producing acts include what is called drafting and the subsequent act of revising what has been drafted to make sure it serves its purpose.

Parallel to these productive acts are the reproductive acts of decoding, or going from the graphic representations either to sound or to silent language. At the same time, the reader seeks to make meaning by summarizing, personalizing, interpreting, or evaluating the text. These responses may take on a further social dimension, which at times can be ritualistic or further dictated by the situation. The responses can range from the tacit act of ignoring the text to the more passive and social acts such as holding an extended discussion of the text. They may also lead to the act of producing another text that responds to, glosses, or comments upon the text just read.

Each of these models of text and the acts related to texts derives from the perceived function of the literate act in a given social context. The novel grew up and developed in a time when people had the leisure to read and had little other access to entertainment. The newspaper also developed a format that enabled it to be read easily in various places, particularly trains. The scholarly paper developed a format that was appropriate to the research library and a limited number of journals. At times, of course, the model has become divorced from the function; at times, too, the model tends to force a particular functional use upon the writer or reader. The model of the scholarly article in some fields is explained by a style sheet rather than by a discussion of the rules of evidence and proof in the discipline. It is also much too long for a world in which information has proliferated and is needed quickly. It is, therefore, being replaced by the abstract. Similarly, the four-page letter in direct-mail advertising becomes a constraint placed on the advertiser rather than being seen as a way of establishing a rapport with a reader. Both of these examples of models may be vestigial rather than functional.

One may well agree that all of these models of text and of the acts involved in composing or reading and responding are highly conventional but probably functional. One could probably argue that in this respect literacy is not unlike wood cutting, where much of what is done comes from the perceived functions of cutting and splitting modified by the demands for safety and productivity. These then take on a social aspect. So too with many of the functions of literacy within a society. Convention and need dictate the occasions for writing or reading as well as the functions and demand of discourse appropriate to those occasions. It is a convention to write a thank-you letter after a visit, and this convention imposes constraints upon the content and form of the letter. The need for public records of meetings imposes a demand for minutes, and the form is often that dictated by the potential for a lawsuit.

From convention and need the writer or the reader then applies knowledge of both the content and form appropriate to a function on a particular occasion and conducts the appropriate search of the long-term memory. The writer goes on to certain text-producing as well as discourse-producing activities. The text-producing activities include the more mechanical or physical; the discourse-producing activities include those related to the selection and arrangement of content. The reader goes on to both decoding activities and types of response to the text material ranging from discarding to committing to memory to critical analysis. Again, these activities are bounded by social convention and interact with text models. Within the scribal world, these activities help define rhetorical and interpretive communities. Such communities appear to exercise great control on the individual but some are more or less tolerant of deviation. A learned journal style is much more rigid than is that of a general-interest magazine.

Text models exist in readers' heads, and these models form the basis both for their acceptance of particular texts into an appropriate generic group ("this is an essay," "this is an interpretation") and their evaluation of the sufficiency of the text to the model ("this is a *good* essay, "this is a *valid* interpretation"). Such text models appear to be culturally specific, and they appear to affect the rating of student writing and to impose themselves as models on students and thus get passed on from generation to generation. They are used in the gatekeeping role of academic assessment of literacy, and they exert an influence upon who is admitted to the community and, thereby, upon student beliefs and ultimately upon their actual writing performance. These models of text derive from the sociocognitive models of the functions of academic literacy that pervade an educational system. The origins of our current models may be obscure but they were probably born of necessity rather than caprice. We wonder if the five-paragraph theme became popular because it could be written in a single hour's sitting. Once in the system, the models are often difficult to change.

The idea of mental models, their conventionality, and the control they exert upon writers and readers is not new; it goes back as far as Aristotle's *Poetics*, but in many cases the models for specific kinds of texts have not been well elaborated, and the result is that literates and their teachers and judges operate in a world that is ill-defined and therefore not easy to learn to manipulate. We are unclear how the various aspects of text models coalesce in a given situation such as a classroom essay, a final examination, a summary of an experiment, or the like. We are also unclear how these specific exemplifications differ from a shopping list, the telephone directory, a letter from a grandparent, or a notice from the municipality. Furthermore, we are unsure how each of these manifestations serves its particular social and discursive functions. When we know more about these matters, the literacy curriculum becomes much easier to present to students.

Much of our work over the past years has sought to devise teaching strategies that will make the array of models apparent to children and adults. Such an approach differs from current instructional practice because it approaches literacy as beginning with the knowledge of the functional and textual models of our society; it is this knowledge that underlies the ability to participate in a complex activity rather than a set of basic technical skills (which are only aspects of operation within that system). It is this approach that underlies the activities detailed in Chapters 2, 3, 4, and 5 of the student text. The variety of activities and forms stems from a sense of the variety of models that need to be tried and practiced by any student.

THE WRITING CLASSROOM

Teachers and students operate by models even though they are not clear about them. Students often see good writing in terms of inscribing (e.g., neatness and spelling) rather than discourse (structure and style) and reading in terms of decoding the sounds rather than making meaning; such is particularly the case of students who are not successful in schools. Teachers often label students "remedial," "marginal," or "at risk," labels given by the judges, not the judged.

Teachers of literacy and composition at any level need to be honest about the social and cultural nature of writing and its dependence on functional models that produce formal ones. We need to be explicit about these aspects of text and literacy. We would urge an approach to literacy education that brings the whole textual and hypertextual world into the school and places school literacy into a broader context and that directly confronts the sociocultural nature of models of literacy and of text.

In the student text we suggest that the curriculum should be bound to the concept of text in its myriad forms: All forms of text from graffiti to epic poems, from cereal boxes to telephone books should become part of the curriculum and should be explored in terms of their functions and forms. Academic literacy has become overly separated from real-world literacy and made a value in its own right. We and our students need to see academic texts in the broad social matrix of junk mail, business letters, computer programs, greeting cards, rock music on the Internet, and gothic romances.

We and our students should explore this world as a fascinating human world in which the various functional needs to store and retrieve information in print and electronically in order to serve particular rhetorical and social purposes has brought forth a complex array of textual models to meet those needs. We can explore how the models succeed and where they fall short of their end; they can explore the human drama in creating this complex web of worlds that exist on paper and on the computer screen. It can be exciting and challenging, and it can have the payoff of bringing those who have been marginalized by academic literacy into the scribal society.

What does this new classroom look like? To some it will resemble a workshop or a studio where a number of painters or sculptors are working on their own projects, occasionally stopping to examine the work of one person or the painting by a master. There is a constant interplay of the creative and the contemplative. All are working on their material. All are working toward the creation of their portfolio.

Another view of the classroom would be that of a set of networked terminals, where students are working on their writing and are then able to communicate across the space by sharing what they have written on the screen. The classroom can conceivably be a network of individual rooms across a wide space.

During most of the time in the classroom, students are working on their writing and their portfolios. The teacher is not lecturing them about writing or reading to them or giving them spelling drills. There should be times for pausing and sharing and commenting on each other's work. There may very well be time to bring in an essay or a story or a poem for group discussion. These common experiences are ones for the students to share and to be used as prompts for their own writing, either critical or creative.

When you are working in such a classroom, you are serving as the coach and the helper and the monitor. You are observing what each student is doing, setting up conference sessions and groupings. At the same time, you are helping them set up a workshop atmosphere with their own work.

Your classroom is a resource room, both human and material. The resources include you and the students, to be sure, but there are also books, newspapers, dictionaries, thesauruses, magazines, files of various sorts with magazine articles, picture files, and other materials that you and they have gathered. There should be worktables and space for conferences. There should be at least one computer with a word-processing program and a graphics program available. It would be nice to have a modem and access to several databases; it would be even nicer to have a series of networked computers, a VCR or a video-disk player, and a CD-ROM port. These will come to many classrooms and are already available in some.

One clear problem in many settings is that the writing classroom is only yours for an hour a day or less. In this situation, the workshop atmosphere is less easy to set up. It can be done, however, if you are willing to work at it and let the class time be a sharing time and the work time be on the students' own time. In that case, some of the visible signs of work will differ from that in the classroom that is yours to shape physically. You will have to create a mental workshop.

This is done by engendering in the students from the very first day the idea that writing is a social and a communal activity even though there are times when the student has to struggle alone to find the words or images to put on the page or the screen. The communal activities take place in the planning, sharing of work in progress, editing, and preparing of final manuscript or copy. Just as we worked together and with a host of editors, some electronic, some human, so will your students. Writing in this sense is collaborative. It will be especially so if two or more students decide to work on a project or coauthor a report, a story, or a mixed-media creation. Perhaps they need some of the class time to go off together because it is the only time together they will have. Let them go.

The class time is the students' time, not yours. You set it up for them; you establish the goals and constraints; you set some or many of the assignments; you provide feedback as the students are working on their drafts. But, ideally, the class time is a time when they and you are working on their writing together. It is during this time that you do a lot of the reading and commenting on student work in progress; you don't have to take a pile of papers home with you every night or once a week. You can set up peer working groups as well as the grouping partners that we mentioned in Chapter 1.

It is likely that you will need to "train" students to work effectively in these groups. Inexperienced writers (and writing-group participants) tend to ask questions such as, "What do you think of this piece? or "Do you like it?" or "What's wrong with it?" or "Will you fix it?" These are questions a patient asks a doctor. But you aren't a doctor; you do not have all the answers, and the students need to take care of their own writing.

Better questions get better answers. Group time is limited, so it is in everyone's interest to make the most of it. You might require each student to come to a portfolio or writing-group session with two or three specific questions about his or her own work. If a student has a piece of writing by another student, he or she might have two or three specific questions about that as well.

The questions can be response questions, such as "How does the passage make you feel?" "Do you like (name of character)?" The questions can also be technical: "What do you see as the progression of images in this piece?" "What else can I tell you to make the idea more acceptable?" "Does the metaphor or analogy make sense throughout the piece?" "Do you think the tone is even?"

In the portfolio group, where people are considering several pieces and their own and others' progress, the conference should also be one where everyone is prepared to speak, not to be interrogated. You can hand out a report form for each of them to bring:

1. I'm working on _____.
2. Here's where I am now (include the decisions already made).
3. Here's what I'm going to do next.
4. I have questions about (or problems with) _____.

In this way, each writer is the primary audience of his or her own progress report, as well as the initiator of the conversation about a specific piece of writing. After the writer's report, the group members can move to the text of the piece reported on or to the whole portfolio.

This same format can be used for conferences with you. In two minutes each, students can bring you up to date with work on one or two pieces or a project; in four or five minutes, you can get a progress report on the portfolio as a whole. The whole is helpful and efficient, and the center of the class time remains on the students and their portfolio.

For some of us, shifting to this sort of classroom is not easy. We love the sound of our own voices; we love being the expert. But, as we said in Chapter 1, the point is surrendering our control and giving it to the students.

Chapter 3   Getting Started: Goal Setting and Monitoring

Planning a course in composition (or any subject, for that matter) involves considering how student performance will be judged. Even when we choose our textbooks, we are subconsciously considering how students will be graded and judged. At times, we throw up our hands in despair and postpone thinking about the inevitable; then we step in at the end and blindly grade. At the same time, we rail against those tests that give grade or age levels to what our students do as being insufficient indices. We might deride as ridiculous the claim by some teachers that they can tell the difference between a composition with a mark of 77 and one with a mark of 79. Some among us argue that we cannot even talk about the quality of our students' performance; we can only describe it. They say that "Who is best?" or "How good are we?" are the wrong questions.

Are we perhaps fooling ourselves when we go to these extremes? Don't we make judgments of quality when we look at what our students do day in and day out? Don't we often say this student is better than that or this work is better than we would have expected. Most teachers do indeed have standards by which they judge students or themselves. We believe that the makers of most large assessments also have sets of standards. Clearly one set of standards concerns what it is we choose to look at, which is to say what test questions we set or what paper assignments we make. We also have standards about what is appropriate learning. A student may say, "I have written these papers," and we will reply, "Fine, but you should write these." When we make up a test, we choose to include a measure of editing or spelling or to omit it; we choose to set or not set a topic for composition. We decide to include or exclude questions concerning interests or habits or preferences. All of these decisions we make because we have ideas concerning what is important, what indicates the quality of the program or the student. All of these decisions come from an implicit set of standards that most of us have in our heads. We should make those standards explicit to students from the very beginning of instruction. This is the main point behind the idea of portfolios, as we mentioned in Chapter 1. Getting down to brass tacks with standards is the subject of this chapter.

In portfolio classrooms, each student gathers a collection of materials, both trial attempts and finished products, in order to show the broad accomplishments of the student. The range of materials has theoretically been broad, but in practice it has comprised mostly written records, either compositions by the student or some sort of log of activities recorded by student or instructor. The portfolio has been heralded as a good way of monitoring "student progress." It has also been promoted as a means to show the nature and quality of a school's program. Some of the advocates of portfolios have questioned whether they can be used for any sort of summary judgment of the performance of large groups of students—the purpose that rules most tests and assessment programs. That is not our concern, rather we are concerned with the class and the individual student.

Students and parents as well as policy-makers and the taxpayers have a vested interest in knowing the value of their investment in education. We can't deny their legitimate concerns. Nonetheless, we should give them an answer that respects both their legitimate interest and our sense of the complexity of what we do as teachers of writing, whether in our classrooms or for the community at large.

AN INDUCTIVE APPROACH TO QUALITY AND STANDARDS

When setting up a writing course or program, a good first step is to address three broad questions about standards and assessment. The first is whether and how one student can write "better" than another; the answer to this question will say something about the nature of our inherent standards. The second is in what ways a student in the twelfth year of school or second year of college should be better or different from a student who has been in school only six or nine years or has just entered the system; the answer to this question will also help us define our standards, particularly with respect to our curricula and programs. The third question is what should be done with the student who has demonstrated mastery of these standards; why continue repeating the activity over and over? We have found that many of us have standards of quality and of maturity, but we do not articulate them. Asking these questions carefully and thoughtfully can help us articulate our standards and prepare us to share them with our students, who must know what they are in order to prepare their papers and their portfolios. It doesn't help them to go through a course in composition only to be told, "Well, you didn't do it [whatever the *it* may be] well enough or often enough." In suggesting ways for you to consider these questions, we have asked many of our colleagues these questions and gone over various syllabi and course outlines. Our general answers cannot replace your specific ones. You must go through this exercise yourself in order to find out what you believe.

Question 1:   What Is Being Better at It?

We would group the various responses according to three broad categories, which correspond to what we have elsewhere found to be the major aspects of the domain of language and composition learning: *knowledge*—what we as instructors expect students to know that they might not have otherwise known had they not come to school (which is to say the content of the curriculum); *practice*—what we want them to learn to do in reading and writing and literature; and *habits*—the ways in which we want them to behave and the attitudes and dispositions we want them to have. That these three emerge results from the fact that although the range of English curricula has been characterized as having differing ends (characterized by such terms as *heritage*, with its focus on knowledge, *skills*, with its focus on practice, and *growth*, with its focus on preferences), in practice, few schools or instructors are so ideologically committed that they pay much attention to any one of the three.

Another way of looking at the curricular issue is to see that the various debates concern specific items of knowledge, specific kinds of practices or skills, and specific kinds of habits or preferences; these debates operate within a generally shared set of standards that can be summarized as follows: We want to fashion students into an image of the individual who is committed to literacy and the best uses of the language; who is knowledgeable, articulate, fluent, and flexible in adapting to a variety of literary and literate situations; who is open and gregarious; who is, in sum, the kind of scribe we outlined in the previous chapter. This kind of "good writer" is also a reader.

A great part of the knowledge base for writing comprises the books or other selections read. "With commitment comes knowledge both of texts and of text conventions and procedures. Upon these two are built the practices of reading, responding to what is read, and transferring what is gained to writing," some instructors have reported, supporting by their experience what we have set forth as theory in the preceding chapter. Most of the models that guide our writing and the writing of our students have been derived from prior experience, that is to say, from reading and viewing. It seems clear that it is not simply a matter of quantity; there are a number of books that instructors think students should have read. This is what has come to be called the *canon*, a complex concept wrapped in a number of values and value judgments both about particular writers and texts and about the criteria by which those writers and texts are selected. Within the group of teachers of English there are frankly many conflicts and contradictions, and we do not advocate a particular canon. But we know that canons exist in instructors' heads and in the heads of those who criticize and support them.

The second kind of knowledge that a better student possesses consists of the various terms and concepts by which people talk and write about what they read ("knowledge of conventions," in the phrase most often used). These are often defined by the critical terms contained within handbooks and glossaries of textbooks, but instructors see their importance in use, not simply as passive learning. Students should also be knowledgeable about the conventions of oral and, particularly, written discourse, from spelling and penmanship to margins and bibliographies. It seems clear that having such knowledge marks the quality student, but it is less rote knowledge than applying it in reading and writing that makes a student even better yet, as we pointed out in the previous chapter.

In terms of practice (the talking and writing of and about texts that is the central part of performance in school literature), the better student is the one who can sustain talk longer, can use various literary and discourse concepts and conventions, can supply more details and features of the text to support a position, and can talk about the text at a level of generalization or abstraction that marks the "good" interpreter. Such talk or writing also implies making connections between the given text and, first, personal experience, but later, the stockpile of other texts that have been read or studied, as well as the broad set of cultural artifacts—film, television, music, art—contemporary with the text or with the readers.

What we have described so far carries over into the subdomain of habits; students are expected to prefer reading and writing to other leisure activities and print to other media, to like the approved texts better than the more "common" ones, and to find the academic kind of talk and writing more pleasurable than simply talking about their feelings, recapping the text, or not saying anything about what they have read. We want students to be willing writers, then we want them to be clear and graceful writers. Teachers want students to be sensitive and reflective.

Question 2:   What Are the Differences that Accompany Age or Experience?

What we have been saying about being better carries over into being older. As they grow older, students are expected to have read more and more mature works, works written for a general adult population. They are expected to have read more complex works in structure, tone, or language. They will have the capacity to use more complex models of text and the uses of text. Their stock of references should be broader, and it is clear that they should have acquired a sense of the nature of the major genres, the major literary themes, the major rhetorical devices and tropes. The knowledge is not specialized or detailed, but a broad categorical familiarity is expected through the high school years and into the first years of college.

In the subdomain of practice, it seems generally expected that older students will read and write more "difficult" texts and respond to more stringent demands imposed by the situation of reading and discourse in the classroom. These demands include:

1. amount of background information required;
2. length and elaboration of the discourse;
3. theoretical appropriateness and consistency of the discourse;
4. acknowledgment of alternative positions.

Although one may say that these levels apply to the quality of performance in writing and composition as well as reading and literature, they seem more applicable to change over time and change in the amount of time it takes to do things. They speak to three persistent goals in writing instruction: that students become more articulate in their writing; that they become more fluent in their writing; and that they become more flexible in their writing. Articulateness is seen in the quality of the content, structure, style, and conventions of their writing. Fluency is seen in the ways in which writers adjust to different audiences, situations, and demands. These three are the marks of an adept in almost any medium or art form, from sculpture to rodeo-riding, from programming to writing.

Most instructors expect students who have had more instruction (i.e., are older) to refer to historical and other cultural information more, to use more and more elaborate references to critical terminology, and to refer to more texts that have been presumed read or known. Instructors expect them to use more technical language, to extend their writing or speech, to consider more points, and to write or talk more consistently in terms of their theoretical approach to the text. Instructors also expect the older student to be more aware that other views or interpretations are as valid as the student's own and to recognize the differences among interpretations and to account for them. In writing, instructors expect more elaboration, greater length, more complex syntax, and greater use of language that exhibits tentativeness. One should note that the operating term is the comparative. It is not the response to the task that has changed, but the elaboration surrounding that task. All of this elaboration implies a consequent extension of the amount of time devoted to a single, more complex task. The terms used in the individual response refer to increases in complexity and elaboration rather than qualitative differences in perception or articulation. It appears that younger students may lack certain specific knowledge, particularly of authors and terms. The changes are in complexity and perhaps in level of abstraction, but these changes are neither predictable nor necessarily linear.

More mature preferences and habits tend to follow the same pattern as that of practice. Students are expected to prefer both the more "difficult" text and the more difficult approach to a text or a problem in composition. Not that they give up their simpler taste; they are expected to become more eclectic and diverse in their reading. In addition, students are expected to make more complex value judgments and more subtle distinctions between what they like and what they know is "good." At a high level, they should like the "good" whether it be determined in terms of style or substance.

To summarize the contemporary set of ideas of quality: instructors at all levels want to fashion students into an image of the individual who is committed to literacy and literature; who is knowledgeable, articulate, fluent, and flexible in adapting to a variety of literary and literate situations; who is open and gregarious. As instructors, we shape our curriculum and our teaching to that end; we wish to reproduce ourselves, certainly our best selves. One way of summarizing what we expect can be seen in the following table, which shows what a group of teachers in British Columbia set forth as the answer to their questions about quality and learning.

Table 3.1

Aspects of Types and Levels of Performance in School English

	What's Quality?	What's More Mature?

Knowledge	Having read more
	Reading the right texts to
	    build up background
	    knowledge
	Getting the lingo
	Knowing the conventions
	    and rules
		Having read older
		Knowing genres, themes,
		    and movements
		Getting theory and
		    abstractions

Practice	Saying more
	Reading and writing
	    various text types
	Using the right terms and
	    language
	Using detail
	Finding abstractions
	Making connections
	Being clear
	Being coherent
	Being aware of the
	    audiences
		Reading and writing more
		    complex texts
		Being more consistent
		Being more elaborate
		Increasing the variety
		Making alternatives
		Making more abstract
		    connections
		Including more details

Habits	Choosing reading over
	    other activities
	Choosing the preferable
	    texts
	Choosing to write
	Being willing to share and
	    participate
	Using the resources
	    available
	Being self-critical
	Being reflective
		Choosing more complex
		    texts
		Choosing a greater
		    diversity of texts
		Making more subtle
		    judgments of texts

We don't think that you should take this list over wholesale for your course, but we do think that it is a good starting point.

The best way to plan your class is to ask yourself what you really mean by *quality* and *learning* (or *growth*, or *development*, if you prefer those words). Set those down in a list. Be brutally frank. Then review the list and see if you have both your standards and your marking or scoring guide for your students' work.

After you have done this, share it with the students. They are the goals for your course. The sharing is the most important part of a portfolio-based course.

Question 3:   What Happens to the Student Who Has Achieved "Mastery"?

This last question is one of the mysteries of the curriculum in composition and the language arts generally. It used to be relatively clear that when students had read certain texts or authors, they then moved on to others, just as when they had finished a unit on grammar they had completed work on the sentence. Such was one of the comforting aspects of having a set reading list and a set kind of essay to write. One read and wrote and one was done. Then one could go on to other things—perhaps fishing. As the canon disappeared in the onslaught of the new criticism and reader-response, and as the idea of text models devolved into the idea of the writing process, there was no clear sense of what it meant to complete study. The dominance of practice in writing means that there is not a clear body of knowledge, and an examination of professed standards with respect to practice appears to show that the notion of good, better, and older may be charged with being somewhat vague. The curriculum might explore diversity of media and modes of presentation, a form of enrichment rather than acceleration.

The focus on practice or performance is complicated by the fact that quality is a matter of perception. Assessment, particularly direct assessment of any sort of performance, depends upon judges who set the standards. Occasionally judges may use measuring tools—stopwatches or counters of one form or another—but usually they are left with the human eye and mind. With performance in writing, one confronts the problem of estimating from examples, which are products. Students read and respond to specific texts, and they write specific texts. They spend no time doing generic reading, writing, or literature. Each product is rated by some form of jury (teachers or other parties) as good, poor, or indifferent. Usually the criteria for the judgment are not clearly specified; one has to trust in the jury. We will spend more time on marking and grading in Chapter 5.

Much research has suggested the difficulty in making any estimate of such abstractions as ability or competence from examples. In other fields—such as ice dancing or dressage—this problem has been long recognized; they talk of someone being "good" with the realization that the estimate is based on a recent performance judged by someone who has been certified as a judge (although not any the less fallible for being so). The rating is not viewed as a capacity that will stand the next test. Participants and judges know what constitute the major dimensions of good performance, but they do not necessarily talk about generic dressage. A person achieves a standing in the field after a great number of assessments by different judges. So it should be with the language arts and literature learning. Each rated product should be an exemplar of a student's performance, not an index of ability. That is where the portfolio comes in.

USING THE PORTFOLIO FOR GOAL-SETTING

Since assessment is tied to instruction and is based on exemplars, an accumulation of heterogeneous material is needed in order to make any meaningful estimate of a student's performance as a reader or writer. That's a fancy way of saying you can't judge a basket of apples by looking at only one apple. This is where the portfolio comes in. An exemplar is a specific performance or product that has been rated and that can possibly be related to a performance level. A typical exemplar would be a composition about a novel that has been rated by an instructor or some other juror. The juror has said that the composition is excellent work for a high-school sophomore and has remarked on the content, organization, style, and use of conventions of writing. That rating cannot be generalized to an assertion about the level of ability or the competence of the student as a reader or writer. Nor can it be used to make more than a tentative assertion about a presumed capacity such as articulating a reasoned response to a text. It is but a small piece of the mosaic, a provisional judgment of a performance at a given moment in the history of an individual, often in reference to a limited sample of other individuals, and subject to revision. The students are not good or poor readers or writers. They have written *this* task well or had trouble answering *this* question on *this* passage.

When one looks at exemplars and judges them, when one uses such terms as *well* or *trouble*, one should also be aware of one's limitations as a judge. Judges look at things or people and rate them according to mental models of what the thing or the person should look or act or taste or smell or feel like. Judges do not rate objects or people but perceptions. They rate what they perceive. What they perceive is colored by sets of cultural or communal norms of appearance or behavior.

In writing, some cultures value content and others style. Some classes expect neatness and handwriting; others expect creativity and the use of computers and mixed media. How a student does, then, depends upon what the judge expects and demands. Usually that is where you and your set of expectations and goals come in. The performance is not a good exemplar, but it is only what you and your colleagues (either fellow teachers or students) perceive and acknowledge as good. Each judge must make clear the criteria, and this is something that many instructors in the language arts do not do; they know good writing when they see it, but they keep the criteria up their sleeve. We are not blaming them; a lot of grading has been done that way in the past. But it is unfair to the students. That's why so many students will ask, "But what do *you* want?" and then be crushed when they don't get a clear answer.

If you realize that you are, indeed, dealing with the perception of exemplars, rated according to standards that have been made explicit, you can say to a student: "You are not 'done'; there is another exemplar that you need to try, one that we believe is more difficult." The task changes, the text changes, the context changes, and the focus on a dimension changes. Each change or set of changes makes the task more difficult and new; it produces a different exemplar that we can rate and perhaps compare to earlier exemplars. In a sense, then, mastery is never accomplished; all have more to learn; there is always the next book or paper to be scrutinized by someone else. Given this line of reasoning, the portfolio becomes the accumulation of exemplars that allows someone to *begin* to make some sort of summary assessment of the individual as a reader or writer. That is its importance; it is also part of its limitation. The portfolio presents the same sort of problem for assessment that is presented in literature by the canon. In literature, the canon is that set of texts or principles for selecting texts that an individual or group has employed as a sorting mechanism. It includes and excludes, and it is arbitrary and results from ideology. The same thing can be said of a portfolio. It is ideologically based in its selection of exemplars and the criteria for their selection. That is why you must help the students shape their portfolios and not simply create your class portfolio. If the portfolio is theirs and well-reasoned, it can be used in a variety of situations and contexts, from admission to college or graduate school to access to a job.

TURNING THEORY INTO PRACTICE

From what we have argued so far in this chapter, it would seem a relatively simple step to plan the instructional year. At the same time, it is complex and requires your thinking through a number of questions:

1. What specifically are your criteria for good or superior performance in writing?
2. What changes in knowledge, practice, and habits do you expect to see and what changes do you want to see?
3. What are the points of negotiation and where is the room for individual student goal-setting?
4. What sorts of evidence for performance and change do you consider minimal?

Answering these questions before the class begins is a good way to draft your syllabus or course outline. The first one lets you and your students know what it is you mean by good writing. The second sets forth the general areas of emphasis that should dominate your assignments and classroom activities. If these changes are important to you, then they are the ones upon which you and your students should spend the most time. In a sense, when you answer the first two questions, you have set forth your goals and you have even drafted your final examination or project.

The third question, however, changes the focus somewhat. In asking this question, you are letting your students into the act. You are recognizing the fact that they might have specific aims within your broad set of goals and objectives. Some students might want to get over their fear of writing or getting started; some might want to learn more about specific tricks of the writer's trade; some might want to understand more about language and its effect on readers; some might want to get by—however they define getting by. Here is where you need to let the students set their goals and begin the delicate process of negotiating where they want to go in their writing (or not go, as the case may be) in light of what you aim for in your instruction.

In thinking in terms of a portfolio and exemplars, you have the framework for negotiation. What sorts of things do they and you think would be the best exemplars of their goals and your objectives? How many different sorts of items do you want? How many do they think they should put in? What do they want to put on exhibition?

How do they think it should be judged? In working through these questions during the course of the year, you and they have the chance to continue that negotiation. We have outlined the negotiation from the student's perspective in Chapter 1 of the student text. Your starting point needs to be as clearly articulated.

MONITORING PROGRESS

Once you have established a set of goals for the class and enabled the students to set forth their goals and objectives for the creation of their portfolios, the work of the class can begin in earnest.

But you should not be seduced into thinking that once you and they have set the goals, they remain fixed in concrete. We often revise our goals and objectives, and we often need to set new ones. We have found in our experience that it is useful to have the students review their goals every four weeks or so. We will use a form like the one set out below.

GOAL PROGRESS REVIEW

Name:

Date:

Goal that I set for myself:

What have I accomplished toward this goal?

What more do I need to do to reach it?

Changes in the goal:

New goal that I want to set:

It is best to use one form with each goal. It is also best not to force the students to review each goal every time but to select one that they are particularly happy or unhappy with and review that. Not all of our goals are short-term or long-term. No more are those of our students.

At the end of the course, a review of the beginning-of-the-year goal sheets and the Goal Progress Review forms that have been accumulated over the year can help the students in the writing of their autobiography or introduction to the portfolio.

Chapter 4 Organizing the Sequence of a Writing Course and Making Assignments

So far in this volume we have set forth the logic of portfolios and made a case for them in writing instruction and pedagogy, and we have described what is involved in being a writer so that you might outline a course into which the book we have written may fit. We have spent some time on goal setting for you and your students. Now when we turn to the matter of sequence and the specific assignments that are covered in Chapters 2, 3, 4, and 5 of the student text, we will again start with a few premises that come from the place where we think instruction should start, assessment.

1.   Written composition is an ill-defined domain. By this we mean that there is a lot of argument about what should go on in a writing course. There is much ink spilt on process and product, on critical inquiry and liberation.

2.   Written composition is a domain in which products are clearly the most important manifestation; the texts that students produce form the basis for judgments concerning those students. Teachers and assessors know that and so do students. It's what is written that counts.

3.   These products are culturally embedded, and written composition is a culturally embedded activity. The culture may be fairly broad or it may be relatively narrow, such as the culture of a specific rhetorical community, but students inhabit and produce compositions that reflect those cultures.

4.   When a student writes something in many courses and examinations, what is usually written is a first draft of an assignment that the student has only seen on the day of the assessment; that draft is then rated by a group of people who make a judgment as to its quality. The result is an index of PDQ, Perceived Drafting Quality. Whether PDQ has any relation to writing performance or ability is unclear, although it is probably a fair index.

5.   Given the fact that what is assessed is PDQ, it is little wonder that students see writing performance as comprising adequacy of content, handwriting, spelling, grammar, and neatness. Such is the case of the reports of secondary school and first-year college students in many countries of the world as to the most important features of the textual products of a school culture.

6.   If we want to remedy that situation, then there must be a clearer relationship between the nature and form of assessment and the curriculum in written composition.

If these then comprise our description of the general situation with respect to writing and its assessment and teaching, how do we propose helping you to establish courses to deal with these problems? The answer comes, we think, from the two principles of portfolio assessment that we have stressed.

1. We believe that it is important for instructors to insure that they are getting a representative sample of student writing and that they disclose their criteria and assumptions about good writing.

2. In order to achieve this end, we think that the best sort of assessment and, by extension, instruction is one that gathers a wide sample of student writing, preferably writing performance that allows one to judge articulateness, fluency, and flexibility. Just as in the judgment of a competition like gymnastics or ice skating, the judges view compulsory figures, short programs, and long programs—thus allowing a balanced view of performance across a range of exemplars—so, too, should writing assessment assess across the domain using a sufficient number of examples to make a balanced and meaningful judgment of both the individual student and the writing program whence that student came.

Consider the fact that when an instructor decides upon a grade for a student after a semester or a year, that instructor consults a grade book or some other cumulative record. That record comprises several estimates of the student's performance, usually on the basis of five or six writing tasks that are varied in length and form and demand and on the basis of several exercises and other aspects of classroom performance. At its best, the estimate is cumulative and balanced. The instructor can scan it and see whether the student has improved, whether there are still areas of weakness or imbalance of strength, and whether one student has used the resources of the instructor's feedback better than another. On the basis of all of these considerations, the instructor makes an estimate based on the portfolio of a student's work.

The best instructors have used this sort of assessment, covering a broad segment of the domain and considering the whole portfolio of a student's work. Unfortunately, these same instructors will often accept the estimate of a poorly constructed writing assignment or standardized test over their own cumulative judgment.

So, to the planning of the writing course: Clearly the course must make room for increasing the variety of types of writing that students will practice. We have suggested in Chapter 2 that this variety is determined by the function of the discourse, by the cognitive demand of that discourse, and by the social situation of the discourse.

Functions of Discourse

Expressive—focusing on the author

Referential—focusing on the world

Conative—focusing on the reader

Metalingual—focusing on language

Poetic—focusing on the text as an art object

Phatic—focusing on the channels of communication

Cognitive Demand of Discourse

Reproducing—demanding a representation of given oral or written discourse, as in notes

Reorganizing—demanding a reordering of given information or ideas

Organizing–demanding an ordering of a variety of data that is known

Generating—demanding the creation of both content and the form or structure for that content

Social Contexts of Discourse

Person—who is doing the writing—the individual, a group, a committee?

Time—how much time is there for the writing?

Occasion—is there a social or psychological situation for the writing, such as an examination?

Audience—to whom is the writing addressed?

Outcome—what is expected as a result of the writing, such as an answer, a critique, or the like?

As we plan a writing course, what variety of each of these three conditions can we provide students? Alternatively to providing variety, we might concentrate on a particular function for the writing or a particular sort of occasion for it. Most scientific writing is devoted to organizing and reorganizing in order to represent the subject matter and provide information to a neutral audience that is expected to understand the material. A course in advertising might focus much more on persuasion rather than information, and a course in creative writing is generally concerned with generation of poetic discourse for an unknown audience.

In most "general" writing courses, however, the focus is broader than a single function or cognitive demand; instructors seek to create conditions whereby students may experiment across types and kinds of writing, where they may develop their capacity to move from situation to situation. In these courses, the goal is to help students develop a portfolio that demonstrates their ability to move from situation to situation and from one type of discourse to another.

In addition to presenting a variety of kinds of writing, the course should also explore the variety of approaches to the writer's craft. To revisit the second part of the figure in Chapter 2, we can glimpse this variety:

Surfaces

Paper

Screen

Tape or film

Other (wood, stone, metal, cloth)

Inscribing Instruments

Manual (pencil, calligraphic pen)

Mechanical (typewriter, letterpress)

Electronic

Other (skywriting)

Text-producing Acts

Inscribing

Editing

Discourse-producing Acts

Drafting

Revising

If a class were to take up this variety of tools, surfaces, and acts, the resultant environment would be a workshop. And that is precisely what the portfolio classroom should become. We can best learn to write in an atmosphere where proper exploration with the tools of writing are available and where students can get the feel of what it is to work with a brush on rice paper when writing a letter, as opposed to working with a computer and a layout program. Such a workshop should have the tools to produce a finished text, including the possibility of two-color printing. That would be the ideal, of course, but we have seen this possibility in institutions where the print shop is near the English classroom. The shop serves as the laboratory for the classroom.

In such a classroom, the instructor's role is much more that of the coach that we described in the first two chapters. The instructor becomes a resource person for the students and shows them something of the nature of each of the tools, from the dictionary and the thesaurus to the bindery, from the role of free writing in sharpening the writing muscle to the role of the spell-check in helping edit the final manuscript. In such a workshop, the students may work singly or collaboratively. It will prove that some of them are better at parts of the process of producing a final text than others. *The Writer's Market* lists twenty-two kinds of editor; it would seem reasonable that not every student is equally adept at the job of each of the twenty-two. This is where the classroom as workshop comes into play and where the students may work together to produce the portfolios.

In addition to serving as a guide, the teacher's role is to help make sure that everyone in the classroom is working. At times that may mean cajoling or threatening. At times it may mean giving an assignment or acting as an editor. But your role is not that of the twenty-two editors any more than it is the role of the students. You are the person who is the authority, who knows about writing and about the nature and variety of texts and styles and discourse types. You are the one who sets the tempo and the atmosphere of the writing classroom/workshop.

USING THE STUDENT TEXT

There are dozens of activities and assignments for students in the book, and we will not attempt to provide an "answer key" or list of suggested responses to each one. They are suggestive and illustrative; they are also there for you and the students to adapt. Many of the activities or techniques are followed by examples of student writing. These are not models to be imitated, but they are meant to suggest to your students ways of responding.

Here is one global, all-purpose, one-size-fits-all suggestion: *Ask students to write about every activity they do.*

This may seem obvious, but there are many activities headed "Thinking About." We think these should be thought about with pencil and paper or keyboard and electronic notebook. "Think about three goals" is not the same as "Write three goals," but thinking in writing will help solidify the thinking even if the students never show what they have written to anybody.

The following are suggestions for activities in each chapter of the student text.

Chapter 1

Ask students to write responses to the **THINKING ABOUT...** questions about product, process, goals, etc. They might share these in class to get some ideas from each other.

The planning sheet in Table 1.1 on page 16 should also be filled out, even though it may change fifty times between the beginning and end of the course. The portfolio is a work in progress, and the continued development of the plan is an important feature.

Chapter 2

For early writings, students should answer the **THINKING ABOUT...** questions briefly.

"Opening Moves" (page 31): You might have students try all of these and then pick some that work especially well for them. Working with a writer's notebook could be an ongoing requirement for the course.

Chapter 3

The preview questions for different organizations in Checklists 3.1–3.6 are especially useful for "prevising"—anticipating and planning for the form and content and effect of the piece. A little prevising can save a lot of revising.

As with the portfolio plan, changes are expected. And as with the portfolio plan, changes to a written plan can be better understood than changes made in the air.

Checklist 3.7: This might be done in writing for some pieces. "Yes" and "no" answers are not particularly useful, as they do not reveal the reasoning behind the decisions writers make.

Chapter 4

Completing the research project proposal in Checklist 4.1 gives the student a specific research agenda before she or he goes to the library, the database, or the field for interviews. As with all other plans, it is a working or a draft document. We think it needs to be written.

"One-page Research Paper Assignments": Besides being fun, these are easy entries into the world of research-based writing.

"Assignments for Subject Areas": "Writing for Learning" and "Organizing for Presentation" are categories that overlap. Perhaps they can best be distinguished by time and purpose. "Writing for Learning" activities take five to ten minutes and are meant to begin exploration and understanding. "Organizing for Presentation" activities, besides requiring more time, are meant to show the range and depth of the understandings reached.

Chapter 5

The questions in Checklist 5.1, "Questions Asked about Literature and Its Reading," within or across groups, make excellent prompts for a reading log or journal entries. They can be used throughout the course, as well as in literature or critical theory courses. The same is true of the approaches to reading and writing about literature.

The "Discussion Record" on pages 171–172 should be useful if the outcome of a discussion is important and a record should be written. As an instructor, you can't be present at seven different discussions, but you can read the discussion records and have a feel for what happened in each of them.

Chapter 6

In relation to the **THINKING ABOUT...** features, you might tell the students, "Don't just think about these; write what you're thinking so you can determine if any change is required. Also, you can look at the pattern of your answers and see the direction your revision might take." These same directions can be given for revising the portfolio.

You and your students can adapt Figure 6.1, "First-Draft Evaluation Form," or make up your own to fit specific rubrics or requirements of works you wish to complete.

Chapter 7

For a completed piece, for an intended piece, for a whole class or genre of writing, or for the portfolio, students can select which of these twenty-seven criteria for good writing starting on page 199 do or should apply.

Responses to the "Quality-control Questions" in Checklist 7.1 should be written. In groups, other readers might respond not only to the piece, but also to the writer's responses. Another application is to have each writer pick several questions to which she or he wants responses and then direct responders to those questions.

Chapter 8

Some instructors require a written piece (as an attachment to the portfolio) that explains answers to the questions in Checklist 8.1 (page 214). It is, in effect, a process piece for the entire portfolio.

Again, written answers to the **THINKING ABOUT...** questions on page 222 might help to lead the writer to conclusions and decisions.

You can ask students to map out portfolio organizations with the strategies outlined on pages 222–226 and then pick the one that will work best for their purposes.

CREATING YOUR OWN ASSIGNMENTS

After planning the overall direction of the course and setting up the classroom or workshop, there comes the time when you must make specific writing assignments. Some of these will probably be more carefully planned than others. After all, you want to move back and forth between controlled writing and writing that is freely generated by the students. The assignment you make can have a number of facets. Which ones you choose to emphasize depends upon the circumstances of the assignment that you want to set. Constraints are probably important occasionally to help students learn how to handle pressure situations; at other times, freedom helps them generate their own writing.

A. Instruction—Are there any specific instructions or is there simply a stimulus or a request to write? Sometimes it is useful to present an open assignment like "Write your impressions of the field trip," or "Write about this poem." This is the kind of assignment that helps you and the students find out what they will do when left to their own resources.

B. Stimulus—What sort of material is presented to get the students writing (picture, text, music)? Clearly it makes sense to provide a variety of stimuli. Not all writing is about books or articles; students should try sometime to write about a painting, or a piece of music, or a dance, or a demonstration of a scientific process.

' **C. Cognitive Demand**—What is the level of cognitive processing required? Here we go back to the ideas discussed earlier about whether the assignment calls for reproduction, reorganization, or organization or generation of ideas and structure. Over the course of a year, the assignments should vary among these options.

D. Purpose—What is the rhetorical or discourse function? Does the assignment ask the students to focus on language, on their feelings, on the outside world, on the audience, or on the art form that they are creating? Again, we believe there should be variety.

E. Role—Is the writer to assume a particular role or stance? Is the writer to be personal or objective, to be himself or herself or to take on a specific character? If the writer is to be himself or herself, which self might he or she be: the student, the citizen, the child, the representative of a group?

F. Audience—To whom is the writing addressed? What information about the audience is given? The audience can often be the class and the teacher, since they are the main ones that read the assignment, but there may be other imagined or real audiences, from a person one knows well and with whom there is much shared information to a group of people who are unknown. The audience can also be seen as superior or inferior to the writer or as trusted or suspect.

G. Content—Are there any limits as to the topic or content of the assignment? An assignment can be as open as one we saw on an examination, "Write about whales." It can also be specific as to what aspect of the content is desired. Often students are told to narrow the topic themselves, but in the world outside of school, much of the narrowing has already been done. An accident report calls for a description of where the accident took place and a narrative of what happened during the moments before and after the accident. The topic has been narrowed and the content severely limited.

H. Rhetorical Specification—Is there any specification as to the rhetorical structure of the composition (e.g., description, cause and effect)? This specification is usually thought of as predicting the kind of organization that is expected of the writer. In the student text we spend some time in Chapters 3 and 4 going over typical kinds of organization.

I. Tone and Style—Is there any specification as to the style of the final composition or its tone? These specifications might deal with whether the writer is to be detached or personal or whether he or she is to follow a formal or informal style. *Tone* is usually thought of as dealing with the selection of range of emotions and the degree of involvement with the topic of the paper. *Style* refers to the kind of language (formal or informal). In some cases, the audience suggests the style. If one is writing to a friend, the style and tone will differ from that one uses when writing to an unknown group of examiners. One issue in tone is whether or not to be humorous or sarcastic. In some circumstances, particularly in many academic assignments, humor will not sell.

J. Advance Preparation—Is there any advance work to be done before writing (such as research or a field trip)? Many assignments will give an indication as to whether the writing is to be preceded by some preparation time. Examination assignments, however, usually imply that the preparation has already been done.

K. Length—Is there any stipulation as to length? This is often the question that students will ask. In many situations, a minimum length in words or pages will be set. At times, a maximum will be set as well. As writers mature, they get a sense of how long the typical article or essay should be.

L. Format—Is there any prescription about format (spacing, means of reproduction)? These matters are often most important for formal presentations or submissions for publication. As instructors, you will probably have preferences as to margins and spacing or whether you prefer a particular format or font.

M. Time—Are there any time limits on the assignment? In many assignments, there is a deadline. It can range from minutes to weeks.

N. Draft—Is there any specification as to the number or type of drafts? This specification may be related to time. In most examinations, for example, the limited amount of time prevents students from writing more than one draft. In other types of assignment, however, there may be a specification about an initial outline or a whole procedure of drafting, conferencing, revising, and editing.

O. Criteria—Are the criteria for judgment of completion or of quality specified? Oftentimes, there may be a phrase about "neatness and accuracy" or about the importance of detail. Often, however, the criteria are unspecified, and the students are often blamed for not living up to the unspoken.

These dimensions, then, show some of the boundaries that can be put on a writing assignment or that can be withdrawn from it. We have found that when we omit some of the boundaries, students will often ask about them and force us to specify them or to say that we frankly do not care about length, for example, or about tone.

You should scrutinize the actual assignment you give so as to make sure that it is doing what you want. One way to handle this, particularly early in the course, is to make out a task specification sheet for each composition assignment, so that the students may get used to thinking about the nature of the task they are being asked to do. Often publishers or editors will give such a set of specification to professional writers, so that everyone is clear about what is expected.

One form of the specification sheet might look like the following:

Summary of a text:
Cognitive Demand and Purpose: To organize in order to learn

Task description:
The students will write a summary (approximately 100 words) of a nonliterary text, the length of which is approximately 250–300 words and reading time 5–6 minutes. The student will be advised to write the summary in continuous discourse, using his or her own sentences, not direct quotations. In order to write a consistent and coherent text, the student is allowed to change (vary) the order of paragraphs and sentences in the text, if necessary. The student is not allowed to alter the message of the text.

Content area:
The content of the text should be as common as possible—i.e., not distinctly peculiar to any particular country or culture as to style or content. (Possible content areas: popular science, social sciences, history, biology.)

Content cues:
(a) *Text-type:* The text should be a nonliterary, expository text containing comparisons.
(b) *Structural level:* The text should contain a main idea in each paragraph and also some irrelevant details.
(c) *Cohesion:* The text should be consistent.
(d) *Length:* The length of the text should be 250–300 words.
(e) *Syntax:* Average sentence length should vary from 15 to 20 words.
(f) *Lexicon:* The text should contain mainly abstract words.

Audience:
The audience of the summary would be someone who has not seen the text. (To understand the passage in order to learn its content.)

Structural and procedural cues:
The structure and procedure of the summary will be mainly up to the student. He or she will be advised to write continuous discourse and told not to alter the message. The criteria will be given.

Format:
The task will be given a brief paragraph containing the task, structural cues, and criteria.

Condition and administration:
The student will read the passage silently. The time limit for summarizing will be 30 minutes, including the time for reading. The teacher may not give any assistance.

Criteria:
Adequate conveying of the main point of the text. Organization and structure. Consistency, cohesion, and mechanics.

Instructions:
Summarize the following passage in a single paragraph of continuous prose. In your summary, you should include the major point (underlying idea) made in each paragraph of the original passage.

Your summary will be judged as to how concisely you express the main ideas and how clear your summary is to the reader who has not seen the original.

You have 30 minutes to complete your writing.

Obviously, this is a cumbersome step to do with each assignment, but it works well for the first five or six assignments of a writing course. It also helps to give the format to the students so that they may use it to analyze what it is they are expected to do. If certain parts of an assignment are not specified, the students should make sure that they have free choice. They may even use this kind of checklist with other teachers to make sure that they know what it is that is wanted or expected of them.

The other purpose of such a checklist is for you to check your own assignments. It is important not to get into a rut, and such a checklist can help you assure yourself that you are giving the students the chance to be fluent and flexible.

Chapter 5 Stemming the Flow: Marking and Grading

There is one problem that all writing instructors face with dread. Every year when they plan a new course or a revision of one, they blithely forget about it. But some time in the first month comes the first trickle, which becomes a stream, and then a flood of compositions that students hand in. Each one needs to be looked at, and the students—at least some of them—want their papers returned instantly. It is easy enough to ask the students to write something, but then the instructor has to look at each composition and make some judgment as to its quality and how it might be improved. We can't solve every problem, but we can ease the burden somewhat (or at least ease your guilt).

When instructors (or most other people, for that matter) assess student writing, normally they are looking at two aspects of the student's performance: (1) the ability to produce a legible text (including neatness, spacing, spelling, and basic grammar), and (2) the ability to produce effective discourse (including organization, handling of content, and style).

We have marked thousands of papers in class, and we have participated in various large-scale writing assessments and done research on scoring, so we have come to know something about what good marking and evaluation are. Here are some of our tips.

1. It is not necessary to give detailed comments on every composition nor for every draft. It is better to save the lengthy comments for those compositions that the students have a chance to revise or rewrite. If you have seen a composition through its various stages, you have probably made most of the comments that are going to make any sort of an impression.

2. It is best to give feedback as quickly as possible. Having to wait two or three weeks causes students to lose interest in their writing. The feedback does not have to be extensive or detailed. If you are working with one of a series of drafts of a composition, it is best to focus on one major area where you think there might be improvement. Remember that feedback need not always be written; it can be given in a conference or a brief visit with the student.

3. It is always good to make some positive comment on each composition. The returned composition should not be marked only with corrections and negative comments. There is no reason why you, as instructor, should also be the copy editor. Others can do that job as well as you. A well and critically read paper is not one that is covered with marks.

4. Whenever it is possible, a good way of giving feedback is in a conference or small-group discussion, when the instructor and student can go over a composition together.

5. At various times during instruction, it is good to have the students provide the feedback to each other's writing. They get practice in judging compositions;

they often learn how to improve their own compositions; and they usually give good suggestions for improvement. Most of all and best of all, they save you time.

6.   Whenever you mark or comment upon a composition, you should not focus solely on surface aspects, such as spelling or grammar. These are the aspects of writing that make it readable, but they do not make it meaningful. The ability to produce effective discourse is judged when teachers comment on the quality and scope of the content of the composition, on the organization of the composition, on the style and tone of the composition, and on the personal impression the writing made on the reader.

BEING A READER

You are the writing instructor, of course, but when it comes to your students' papers, you are a reader like many others. There are lots of different kinds of readers in the world, and you should probably try out the various roles.

The Common Reader. This is the person who is not an expert on the subject but comes to composition ready to learn or be amused or interested. The comments of such a reader are often direct: "I don't understand."

The Colleague Reader. This is the person who knows something about the subject and is able to say, "Have you thought about this point?"

The Reviewing Editor: This reader is the one who looks at a raw manuscript and decides whether or not there is something there that should be worked on further to make a masterpiece. Such a reader is concerned with the potential of a piece and can suggest new ways of shaping the material. The tone is usually encouraging.

The Copy Editor and Compositor: This is the reader who comes in near the very end of the process of preparing manuscript and helps get it into final shape before the published version is let forth. This reader may have comments on substance but usually is only concerned with consistency, accuracy, and completeness, as well as with the final appearance of the composition and its layout.

The Reviewer. This reader is the one who looks at a composition for some sort of larger public and makes some sort of pronouncement as to whether the public should pay any attention at all to the writing. The judgment may be of the work in isolation, in relation to the author's other compositions, or in relation to other authors or types of work. This is the person who gives the grade.

The Critic. The reviewer isn't the last reader; we can go back to the common reader, and for many published works these are the people who finally determine one level of worth—the marketplace. But there is the professional critic as well; this reader will look at a composition and seek to locate it historically or culturally, to make connections to other compositions, and to discuss its nature, form, and content. The critic seeks to take a disinterested view of a composition and always accepts it for what it is rather than wishing it were something else.

Which of these readers should you be? All of them. The trick is that you must figure out which role you should take at what time. One way to make the job easier for yourself is to discuss your various reading roles with your students and encourage them to try various roles when they read each other's work.

The point is that you do not spend all your time marking compositions; but you should spend a lot of time reading them and being ready to talk with students about them.

USING STUDENT READERS AND PEER REVIEW

We have mentioned several times in this manual the development and use of peer-review or peer-response groups for composition. These are currently fashionable but are not always easy to set up. Often the students are not sure what they should talk about with each other or what their force or effectiveness is.

We have found that these groups do need training to function effectively as groups. They need to determine what their roles as readers are, what their authority is, and how best to use you. There will need to be a few weeks of practice before they begin to function easily and effectively. The first step, we think, is to have them be aware of the different roles of readers and responders. They are to take on a different role with each other at the time of brainstorming and idea generation than they do at the point where the final portfolios are being worked on. It is a good idea to lay out for them the various kinds of readers and how they might best be helpful at different stages in the preparation of the final composition. Some of them might lay claim to expertise in a particular kind of reading, such as figuring out layout and design or copy editing.

A second step is to have them look through your grading criteria and those of the other reviewers you will be using. We go into this in the next sections of this chapter, but we believe firmly that you should share your specific criteria with the students. Explain the terms, get them to use the language when they are talking about each other's writing. That way, you and they will form a tighter community. One way of keeping them up to the mark is for you to move from editing group to editing group, becoming a member of the group as you go and not simply being the visiting expert, even though the students will try to put you in that role. Nudge, don't bulldoze.

DEVELOPING MARKING CRITERIA AND RUBRICS

When you mark compositions, it is useful to keep the different aspects of your judgment separate and thus be both more specific and more even-handed about applying them so that you give credit where credit is due. As we noted at the beginning of this chapter, people judge writing on the basis of text-level characteristics (what the paper looks like) and discourse-level characteristics (what the paper says). Both are important in a writing course and both are natural to nearly every reader. It is a mistake to think that spelling doesn't count, just as it is a mistake to think that spelling well is a mark of a good writer. The important thing is to separate the two in your mind and in the minds of your students so that you don't and they don't make a fetish of one or the other.

At the discourse level, readers usually distinguish the handling of the content (what is said and how maturely or cogently it is said) from the organization of the paper as a whole and of the paragraphs and from the style or tone that is used. Some readers may also include here their personal reaction to what the writer has said. Even writing instructors are human (even though your students may not think so), and they have firm beliefs about the content of many papers. It is important to state your agreement or your disagreement, but keep that distinct from whether or not you think the students has handled the argument or the topic well.

At the text level, readers may separate grammar, syntax, and usage from punctuation, spelling, and general format (including handwriting). Sometimes matters of grammar are questions of style rather than matters of right and wrong.

One way of distinguishing text-level from discourse-level issues is to prepare a brief form that can be attached to each composition. Don't use it for every draft; rather, use it for a composition when it is at the next to final stage. It can also be good form for a peer-editing group to use on each other's writing so as to see what the consensus judgment of a composition might be. They can use it after the first full draft to give a preliminary estimate of how they think it is going. One version of the form might look like this:

	POOR				EXCELLENT
Discourse-level Qualities					
Quality and development of ideas	1	2	3	4	5
Organization and structure	1	2	3	4	5
Style and tone	1	2	3	4	5
Text-level Qualities					
Grammar and wording	1	2	3	4	5
Spelling and punctuation	1	2	3	4	5
Handwriting and neatness	1	2	3	4	5
My personal reaction	1	2	3	4	5

Comments:

One virtue of this kind of scoring sheet is that it enables instructors to be sure that they are not letting one aspect of a composition overwhelm their judgment of the whole composition. It may be that a student has very good ideas and has organized them well but has used a tone that is inappropriate for what is intended. It may be that another composition is perfectly correct in every way but contains very juvenile and unconsidered ideas given the general level of the student or the class.

By examining the various aspects of writing competence, instructors are able to give their students a balanced perspective on their writing and prepare them for the varied sorts of judgments they will receive later on in life. Instructors from around the world have found that they could use these categories for judging all kinds of writing tasks, from a brief friendly letter to a summary to a narrative, reflective essay, or argument. Certain aspects of writing are more important in some types of writing than they are in others. An effective style and tone become important in an argument; clear organization is important to a description or a narrative; and well-developed ideas are most important in a reflective essay. But to say that one is important is to make that aspect a matter of emphasis; it is not the only consideration.

THIRTEEN CRITERIA FOR ACADEMIC WRITING

You can go beyond broad categories to create much more specific scoring schemes to reflect your norms of good writing. We were able to come up with a specific checklist for the norms that many English instructors who take part in state-wide or national assessments of writing hold in their heads, particularly for the type of writing that is called *academic discourse*. Although the judges of writing may disagree as to whether one composition is better than another, there is a set of broad operating norms for writing, particularly for the sort of writing that we call academic. The differences in judgment occur when one judge decides that one norm is more important than the rest and another selects a different one for particular attention. Since your students will be doing some academic writing, we think it is useful for you look at these norms and share them with your students. There are thirteen specific criteria for academic writing under the three broad rubrics of content, organization, and style and tone.

Content

The content dimension concerns the subject matter of a composition and the way it reflects a writer's manipulation of ideas, objects, and events. There are seven sub-aspects of content, which we might argue can be seen as fulfilling successively stringent criteria for academic writing:

1. *Adequacy of information*. There must be sufficient information to fulfill the assignment, which is to say that the content must match the limits set by the assignment.

2. *Richness of additional information*. There may be additional information drawn from the writer's other reading or experience in the area. That information,

however, must be clearly made relevant to the main focus of the assignment. Digression is not permitted.

3. *Relationships drawn among items of information.* The various discrete predications or subtopics must be shown to be related to each other according to an acceptable principle of grouping (see criterion 9). There can be no unrelated subtopics.

4. *Inferences made beyond the scope of information.* The text is not to be a catalog of information, but there must be some inferences drawn from the various bits of data.

5. *Synthesis.* There should be a drawing together of the inferences into a generalization. Taking criteria 4 and 5 together, a composition should have an optimum of three levels of abstraction from specific to first-order inference to second-order generalization.

6. *Evaluation.* The paper should, in most cases, go beyond the reporting of data and should make a judgment, preferably on rational grounds, concerning the merits of the inferences and the generalization.

7. *Alternatives.* The composition should consider alternative explanations or generalizations and show why the one proposed is superior. The paper should give evidence of an open but decisive mind.

Organization

The organization dimension concerns the optimum structure for the composition as a whole text, as well as the arrangements of its subunits. The organization can be modified according to the conventions of particular academic disciplines, but those have the following common characteristics.

8. *Framing.* The composition needs to have a detectable beginning, middle, and end. Although the generalization need not be at the opening, it should be close to it and should be recapitulated near the end. The actual opening may take a number of appropriate forms. The development or middle must be longer than both opening and closing and may follow one of a number of acceptable formats for grouping.

9. *Grouping.* The information and ideas should be combined rationally, using a temporal, spatial, or classificatory structure. These three can be modified to form different complex structures, such as cause-effect, comparison-contrast, or hypothesis testing.

10. *Unity.* The writer has an obligation to indicate the relationship among the parts that have been grouped. The grouping structure should be signaled with the appropriate lexical items for the selected grouping, and these should be rather more present than absent.

Style/Tone

The style/tone dimension refers to the manner in which the composition is presented and particularly the degree to which the manner approximates the conventional uses of language in academic discourse.

11. *Objectivity.* The writer should use impersonal and detached language. There are some exceptions to this standard, particularly in the more "modern" subgroups of the humanities, but impersonality and detachment are still standard in the sciences and social sciences.

12. *Tentativeness.* There should be an ample number of semantic hedges and qualifiers to indicate that the composition is not dogmatic but a part of the academic scholarly dialogue.

13. *Metalanguage.* The composition should use an adequate number of markers to connect the propositions and the paragraphs. The text should, in this sense, make it easy for the reader to see the intended connections among propositions.

This scheme specifies that implicit model for academic writing that instructors in the U.S. use when they read and judge writing. We have found that it is particularly useful to share these criteria with student writers from all cultures, so that they can see that there are certain cultural norms that American instructors in various fields may well apply to their compositions. We are not claiming that these norms are universally valid or should necessarily be considered as eternally correct, but they are the norms that many writing instructors will use to judge student writing, whether those students be native or nonnative speakers. We have found it particularly useful to share these norms with international students or students in ESL or bilingual programs.

Instructors who have used these marking criteria and have discussed them with their students have found that the students appreciate an honest discussion of what is being looked for in their writing. Some instructors have given their students forms for use in peer evaluation. This has been a particularly effective strategy since it forces the student raters to look at many aspects of their colleagues' compositions.

APPLYING THE PRINCIPLE TO OTHER KINDS OF WRITING

Of course you will not be assigning and marking academic writing all of the time. If you have gotten this far in this manual, you shouldn't even be considering it as the only diet. But you should be able to take this set of criteria and adapt it to a variety of kinds of writing. Let's explore the implications of these criteria in relation to other kinds of writing:

Personal writing: What are the criteria for honesty or expression of personality? Is one of them sincerity? What about language? Should it follow an appositional organization where ideas are related by image or association? Should it be metaphoric?

Fiction: Should student stories meet the traditional criteria of a tight plot and developed characters? How experimental may students be? What if they follow television or other formula writing?

Business Correspondence: Are any personal items allowed? How important are conventions and impersonal language? What sort of organization do I expect?

The important thing to note is the degree to which the specific criteria vary depending upon the type of writing or the situation that is involved. At the same time, the broad outlines of content, organization, and style persist across types of writing.

Clear and honest feedback improves student performance in writing. Together with good assignments and time for planning, clear and consistent feedback that attends to both the text-producing competence and the discourse-producing competence of the student helps more students write better. It also helps make for more accurate and consistent assessment of the entering or completing student.

Chapter 6   Grading the Portfolio: The Final Test

A portfolio of learning in writing, we have argued, is a collection of discrete tasks or exemplars that have been rated by someone and that have been assembled by a student as the summary portrait of that student. The portfolio is the student's property and responsibility.

A portfolio contains not simply works produced by a student but works that have been rated by someone other than the student as well as by the student himself or herself. Each work has usually been scored according to some rubric that establishes a cut-off for acceptable performance in the eyes of the jury. With performance in the language arts, therefore, one confronts the problem of estimating from exemplars, which are products. Your students have read and responded to specific texts, and they have written specific texts, or they have made a tape or a video or acted in a play. They have spent no time doing generic reading and writing. The fact of exemplars complicates any estimate of such abstractions as ability or competence.

Instructors base their assessment on exemplars and can only generalize beyond each exemplar by looking at some aggregate such as the portfolio, but one should beware of simply adding up the pieces to form a total score. To do so may misrepresent the domain of writing and the portfolio approach, since the tasks may have different properties or ask for the exhibition of different skills or attitudes. There needs to be some way of determining the comprehensiveness of the portfolio. An alternative we propose is to work from dimensions. One cannot easily say that someone is "a good student" and then point to a sample of writing without being more specific about what in that piece of writing is good. The idea of dimensions helps us to retain a sense of the multifaceted nature of the domain of writing without confusing the task with the trait. One sample of dimensions that we developed for writing is seen in Table 6.1.

Table 6.1

Dimensions and Standards in Writing

(The letters K for knowledge, P for practice, and H for habit
indicate the classification of each.)

Dimension	Basic	Proficient	Advanced
Presents a readable text that follows conventions (K, P)	Writes legible text with words spelled correctly, sentence boundaries marked; conforms to text model (e.g., letter format with salutation, etc.).	Uses appropriate grammar and syntax with compounds; marks paragraphs clearly; uses graphics appropriately.	Uses complex sentences, varied paragraphs; shows evidence of sense of rhythm in prose; breaks conventions when a stylistic advantage.
Presents information/ideas clearly (K, P)	Presents thesis, main point, central impression, general feeling.	Uses consistent terms; defines terms and ideas.	Presents ideas with subclasses and multiple parts; presents information, ideas, scenes with words that vivify them.
Presents an effective voice for different audiences (K, P)	Presents a consistent point of view.	Demonstrates audience awareness across text types; selects topic or approach to effect a goal.	Selects topic or approach to catch the reader's interest; notes opposing views and refutes if necessary; uses irony where appropriate.
Uses appropriate structures (K, P)	Manages a simple sequence.	Manages complex sequences; cause-effect, comparison, etc.	Manages support for hypotheses and complex arguments; mixes modes of organization to gain effect.
Elaborates a text with examples, illustrations, etc. (P)	Gives a single example.	Provides multiple details and illustrations.	Uses analogy, metaphor, and varied illustrative devices; where appropriate, develops symbol or vivid diction.
Participates in a community of writers (P, H)	Edits to present an attractive text.	Revises a text on the basis of feedback from others.	Revises voluntarily; seeks forms of publication.
Writes habitually (H)	Uses writing as an aid to memory (lists, notes, etc.); selects a variety of words and grammatical structures.	Writes voluntarily (journals, diaries, letters); selects a variety of topics, voices, genres, etc.	Writes voluntarily in social or community situations; writes in order to play or experiment with writing.

These dimensions clearly show that to judge a student writer you can't work from a single composition, no matter how long. Neither can an outside judge. You need something like a portfolio, and students may be encouraged to examine these dimensions to help them fashion their own portfolios.

The idea of dimensions is rooted in the complexity of an activity, which to be understood and judged must be seen in terms of its interrelated acts and operations and not just in its surface characteristics. An observer can see aspects of several dimensions in the composition that a student writes or in the videotape of a discussion among students. One dimension should cut across exemplars. One dimension of school writing in Table 6.1 is articulateness across types and audiences; another is habitual fluency. But articulateness includes text-level characteristics (e.g., spelling) and discourse-level characteristics (e.g., coherence).

We can say that there are levels of performance within a dimension. A rater can, then, (1) assign ratings of an item or items in the portfolio to one or more dimensions, and (2) assign successful performance on those tasks to levels within a dimension.

The levels of performance within dimensions constitute the *standards* within a dimension, usually set *a priori* based on the collective experience of the judges. This notion of standard levels of performance has a long history in such fields as gymnastics or dressage. It has a shorter history in academic subjects.

If one accepts the idea of dimensions, the next question is whether one can be more precise about standards for a portfolio within those dimensions. One can if one follows the logic set out below.

In a portfolio, there exists a set of completed tasks that may have been set for the student either by the student himself or herself or by an instructor or assessor. These tasks are individually juried by an instructor or another student as to whether they are satisfactory or not.

Each task can be assigned to one or more dimensions, which are used to assure that the portfolio is multidimensional.

Each of a student's tasks can then be imputed to have met a given level of performance. The division between levels is standard, which is the criterion by which an individual or group is said to have moved from one level to another. Thus, the line between "Basic" and "Proficient" is the standard by which it is determined that a student or group of students might be classified as either basic or proficient.

We present Table 6.1 as an example of the way in which dimensions can help you and your students judge a portfolio. What we have in the various blocks should be thought of as illustrative, and you need to adapt them for your purposes.

If this seems too cut and dried and neat, don't worry; it isn't. As we set forth in the student text (Chapter 8), there are many different ways of shaping a portfolio. The final portfolio consists of a number of works that have already been scored and rated. But the final portfolio is more than the sum of its parts. It has a shape and a pattern and an integrity of its own. That, too, must be judged as an artistic or rhetorical creation in its own right. The package needs to be assessed as much as its contents.

The assessments form a different kind of abstraction from the narrative responses to the questions we posed in Chapter 3 about setting standards (what is better? what is older?) and a different abstraction from the traditional grade. Certainly, of course, a grade can emerge from this sort of assessment of the portfolio.

DEALING WITH AGE AND GRADE DIFFERENCE IN SETTING STANDARDS

The implication of the approach we propose is that it is quite possible to develop a set of standards that enables one to relate the performance of ninth-grade students to that of college sophomores to the extent that similar tasks or items are given to each group. The reasoning behind this approach is that the standards within the dimensions of reading and writing may be seen as continua from basic to advanced. The continua are determined by what research and experience tell us about expected performance and the sequence of the curriculum as it is normally carried out. We believe that the standards we have suggested appear to hold across grade differences and that it would be wrong to set age-specific standards. Our experience teaching at various levels suggests that the variability of student performance according to standards such as these is not age- or grade-dependent. It may be related to development, learning, or instruction, but performance at the basic, proficient, or advanced level as described in these dimensions occurs in secondary as well as elementary classrooms.

The differences between ages are contextualized in the task, but the type of task, the dimensions, and the standards of performance remain. The contextualization of the task corresponds to what in other fields is the difficulty level of that task. In a field such as show jumping, for example, once jumps of three feet have been mastered, the jumps are raised to four feet. A similar phenomenon occurs in writing: A narrative may be a simple first-person chain of events or a complicated exercise in "magical realism"; an essay may be a simple exposition or a complex argument. But despite these changes, certain dimensions remain important at every level (convincingness and coherence in the narrative and clarity and use of examples in the essay, for example). The standards remain similar; the degrees of complexity of the text and the elaboration and abstraction of the response would vary.

THE USE OF DIMENSIONS IN REPORTING

One tends to forget the myriad ways in which instructors report their judgments of students or the various audiences to whom they communicate those judgments. Conversations in the staff lounge, phone calls, meetings, and professional days are some of the ways instructors exchange information about students; but insufficient time to support the process of assessment and the communication thereof leaves them feeling frantic and frustrated. The network between and among instructors, students, parents, and administrators features the range of nonverbal, verbal (informal and formal), and written (semiformal and formal) communication. The forms of communication range from the nonverbal to the formal written report, and the audiences range from the students themselves to the various levels of administration, as well as prospective employers or admissions officers at other institutions.

It is clear that if an instructor or a school adopts a portfolio assessment, the kind of numerical or letter grade that has been the standard in secondary schools and is often recommended for primary grades becomes anomalous. It is senseless to reduce a complex and ongoing assessment to a set of numbers. Given the complexity of the assessment and the variety of audiences that must be served through either formal or informal reports, a system like that we have proposed makes sense for the kind of discussion that goes on in staff meetings about a student or in parent-instructor conferences.

Dimensions and standards also serve as a format for final reports and the reflective statements that serve to introduce portfolios, since they do not pit one student against another but each student against a set of standards. This procedure calls for you to prepare some sort of summary report—a written report in which you take on the role of reviewer (or one of a jury of reviewers).

SETTING UP THE PORTFOLIO PRESENTATION

The primary obstacle that you face in implementing such a system is time to conduct, perform, and report the assessment. It cannot be done casually in an evening. The problem is exacerbated for those of you who may face as many as 120 reports to prepare. Instructors with whom we have spoken and who have been involved in portfolio assessment with as many as 120 students have found ways to work with time and to use the students themselves as collaborators who accept responsibility for creating their own portfolios. After all, you and your students have been looking at the work for most of a semester or a year. In looking at the portfolio, you and they are taking a fresh look, but you are not "marking and grading" in the old sense. The obstacle diminishes, and the rewards of a fair and complex assessment with clear standards and multiple performances are well worth any loss of time; in fact, the assessment time becomes instructional time as well, and the two are no longer separated for instructor or student.

One increasingly popular way of handling the task is to have a week set aside for portfolio presentations. This week takes the place of final exam week, perhaps. In different situations, the presentations have been handled differently. In some schools, they become an all-school event, with each student presenting her or his portfolio with a twenty-minute oral presentation, followed by a chance for group inspection. In most college classrooms, this is not feasible, and a more modest presentation needs to be set up. One way is to have two or three days per class devoted to a display of portfolios for all to see and comment upon. The open display is also possible in classrooms where the portfolios are on disk and the computers are networked so that all can see what is on the screen.

The point is that the display is a formal and public event. It is the time when the students are showing themselves and what they have done to the world. The world can be as small as the class or as large as the school or the general public. But it is a world that can be both interested and, at times, harsh. Often it will be polite but silent in its condemnation. Comparisons will be made. Your job is to help insure that the comparisons will be given and taken well. Not everyone is going to be the most fluid writer. Not everyone is going to be the great researcher. But each can present his or her portfolio in such a way as to show what he or she has accomplished.

This is best done through the self-statement, the catalog, the autobiography, the portfolio cover, and the introduction (however you choose to describe it). This is where the students say who they are, what they know, what they can do, and what their good habits are. We have spent some time in the student text discussing this with the students. We do not have too much to tell you except that it is useful to set up a framework for them to begin to think about their work. That is why we suggested goal-setting and grouping with the three questions. All of these activities lead the students to become self-aware and reflective about their work. We have found that such awareness comes slowly; it takes most of a year for younger students.

But it comes, and it should be apparent in the self-description and in the arrangement of the portfolio itself. In one sense, if you have achieved that with the bulk of your students, you may have taught them more than if you get them all to spell "accommodate" or to stop writing "me and him went to the store." Those skills will follow from the sense of self-awareness that is a sense of responsibility about their writing and their learning.

The self-awareness should also come in the whole scene of the portfolio presentation. We have found that many students will dress up for this week. It is, after all, a big thing in their lives. They are going before a jury that will rate their work.

How the jury operates can vary. We have tried having a jury of teachers and older students, a jury of teachers and administrators, a jury of outside people (such as college faculty or professional writers in the community). The jury may be given a scoring sheet or rating form or it may be asked to write a comment on each portfolio.

One rating form that we have seen is presented in Table 6.2.

Table 6.2

Rating Form for Portfolios

Student:

Date:

	Strengths	Areas for Improvement	Overall Rating (1–5)
Presentation and format of the portfolio			
Rationale and explanation			
Evidence of achievement of personal goals			
Strongest example			
Consistency and development			
Technical accomplishment			
Originality and interest			

Other Comments:

Judge (signature and printed name):

This form can be modified in any number of ways, of course, and you should seek to incorporate your goals and objectives as well as your standards into the scoring sheet and the whole procedure. The judges should be encouraged to be independent. You should not push them to agree with each other. After all, critics do disagree with each other, and these should be open and apparent to the students. They should also be aware of the differences in criteria and that these judgments are one-time judgments; they are not signs of eternal praise or damnation. They can loom large in a student's life, especially if they are negative after a whole year's work. There will be hurt feelings. There is not much you can do.

The judging having taken place, you may then consider the issue of a grade. Grading is, of course, the bugbear of the profession. It's a tough job, but somebody has to do it, and it might as well be you. You can get help from the students, and in many portfolio courses, instructors ask the students to propose and justify (in writing) a grade. Nearly all of the time, the students have a good sense of how well they are doing and whether they are working up to potential. We have had to change no more than 10 percent of the grades proposed by our students. The grade, however, does not represent the same thing as the results of the portfolio presentation. In fact, you can ask the students to take into consideration the whole semester or year of their work as well as the final portfolio presentation. This will give them an even better sense of how they have done as students. They are forced to take into consideration where they started and what they have been doing along the way.

The portfolio becomes, then, a way for you and your students to display the complexity of growth and learning in a complex subject like writing. The portfolio is also a vehicle by which you can communicate implicit standards to students. It is important for you to undertake the exercise of exploring what your implicit standards are and to lay them out in narrative and then in tabular form so that you can then communicate with your students both what the standards might be and what sorts of exemplars might be needed to demonstrate that those standards have been met. It is revealing to us to find out what sorts of writers our students are; it is also helpful to our students if they can share in the exercise both to find out what we want and how that can work together with what they want for themselves. The result can be an amazing sense of growth and responsibility as the students become responsible for their own writing and their learning about writing.

REFERENCES AND RESOURCES

These are some of the books on writing that we have found useful in our exploration:

Belanoff, Patricia and M. Dickson, ed. *Portfolios: Process and Product*. Portsmouth, NH: Heinemann Boynton Cook, 1991.

Bolter, Jay David. *Writing Space: The Computer, Hypertext, and the History of Writing*. Hillsdale, NJ: Lawrence Erlbaum Associates, 1991.

Gaur, Albertine. *A History of Writing*. New York: Scribner's, 1985.

Goldberg, Natalie. *Wild Mind: Living the Writer's Life*. New York: Bantam, 1990.

Goldberg, Natalie. *Writing Down the Bones: Freeing the Writer Within*. Boston: Shambhala Publications, 1986.

Heath, Shirley B. *Ways with Words*. New York: Cambridge, 1983.

Lanham, Richard A. *The Electronic Word: Democracy, Technology, and the Arts*. Chicago: University of Chicago Press, 1993.

Martin, Henri-Jean. *The History and Power of Writing*. Translated by Lydia G. Cochrane. Chicago: University of Chicago Press, 1994.

Spandel, Vickie and Rick Stiggins. *Creating Writers: Linking Assessment and Writing Instruction*. White Plains, NY: Longman, 1990.

Stafford, William and Stephen Dunning. *Getting the Knack: Exercises for Student Writers*. Urbana, IL: National Council of Teachers of English, 1993.

ACKNOWLEDGMENTS

Some of the material in this guide and the student text was adapted from previous work. A portion of that work was supported through the National Research Center on the Learning and Teaching of Literature, funded by the United States Department of Education. Among the materials pirated are:

Purves, Alan C. "The Teacher as Reader: An Anatomy." *College English* 46 (1984): 259–265.

Purves, Alan C. "Clothing the Emperor: Towards a Framework Relating Form and Function in Literacy." *Journal of Basic Writing* 10 (1991): 33–53.

Purves, Alan C., A. Crismore, and S. Takala. *How to Write Well in College*. San Diego, CA: Harcourt Brace Jovanovich, 1984.

Purves, Alan C. "Setting Standards in the Language Arts and Literature Classroom and the Implications of Portfolio Assessment." 1.3 (1983): 175–200.